MICHIGAN

On-the-Road Histories

MICHIGAN

David Lee Poremba

Interlink Books

Dedicated to Kyra and Charlie
And, as always, for Kate.

First published in 2006 by

INTERLINK BOOKS
An imprint of Interlink Publishing Group, Inc.
46 Crosby Street, Northampton, Massachusetts 01060
www.interlinkbooks.com

Text copyright © David Lee Poremba, 2006
Book design copyright © Interlink Publishing, 2006

Library of Congress Cataloging-in-Publication Data
Poremba, David Lee.
  Michigan / by David Lee Poremba.
    p. cm.—(On-the-road histories)
  ISBN 1-56656-616-9 (pbk.)
  1. Michigan—History. 2. Michigan—Description and travel. I. Title.
II. Series.
  F566.P67 2005
  977.4—dc22

                                                              2005013839

ISBN 13: 978-1-56656-616-2

Printed and bound in China

*Photos generously provided by the Monroe County Historical Commission, the
Willard Library in Battle Creek, and the Michigan Economic Development
Corporation (www.michigan.org). Title page photo of Bois Blanc Island provided by
Travel Michigan.*

To request our complete 40-page full-color catalog, please call us toll free at
1-800-238-LINK, visit our website at **www.interlinkbooks.com** or write to
Interlink Publishing
46 Crosby Street, Northampton, MA 01060
e-mail: info@interlinkbooks.com

Contents

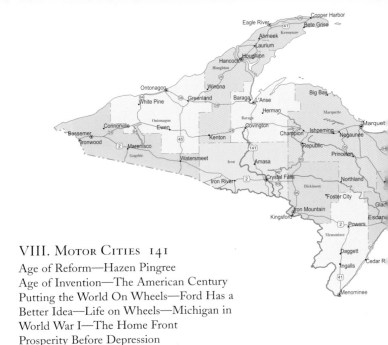

★ **State Capitals**
◉ County Seat
● **Cities 500,000+**
● Cities 100,000-499,999
● Cities 50,000-99,999
• Cities 10,000-49,999
· Cities 0-9,999

h i g a n

	Toll Roads and Bridges		Major Rivers
	Interstate Highways		Intermediate Rivers
	U.S. Highways		Lakes
	State Roads		

0	25 Miles	50 Miles		100 Miles
0	25 KM	50 KM	100 KM	

1

BEFORE THE BLACK ROBES

"If you seek a pleasant peninsula, look about you"—the official state motto encourages both visitors and residents to enjoy their surroundings. And nowhere in the contiguous United States can one enjoy more diverse country. Michigan is one of the most unusual of the 50 states. Split into two large peninsulas, it is surrounded by four of the five Great Lakes and has more than 3,200 miles of coastline, more than the entire Atlantic seaboard of the United States. Its dramatic topography includes roaring waterfalls, the country's tallest sand dunes, vast virgin pine forests, soft rolling countryside, and mile after mile of beaches.

What is now one of nature's more interesting sculptures was once completely covered by a salt water inland ocean. Over a billion years this ocean eventually dried up, leaving mineral deposits across the state from iron ore in the north to salt, gypsum, and lime in the southeast. The area was much warmer then and covered with tropical forests. There was a huge chain of mountains known as the Killarney Range with peaks of up to 25,000 feet in height covering the Upper Peninsula and stretching into Canada. They would all but disappear under the ice sheets that covered the state over a million years ago.

Four powerful, separate ice sheets bulldozed their way across the state, the last one as recent as 11,000 years ago. Billions of tons of ice moving tremendous amounts of gravel, rock, and dirt scoured out depressions that became lakes and lowlands and formed hills and jagged shorelines. The weight of the ice actually pushed the land down, a fact known through scientific studies that show that Michigan is still slowly rising. These glaciers did much to form the Great Lakes and their melt water filled the basins left behind. As the ice slowly receded for the last time 11,000 to 13,000 years ago, the first people moved to Michigan.

9

What they found was a stark land with few trees, some vegetation, caribou, musk ox, mastodon, and a receding field of ice some 5,000 feet high.

PALEO-INDIANS

Not much is known about these first inhabitants of the Great Lakes region but that they were part of the original immigration of people to the western hemisphere. These remote ancestors of modern Native Americans reached North America via a land bridge connecting Siberia with Alaska. They occupied the game-rich northern Great Lakes region and St. Lawrence Valley by about 10,000 BCE. Judging from artifacts uncovered at small, scattered sites, it is assumed that they followed game, hunting with small thrusting lances topped with a very distinctive fluted point made of sandstone. They carried other tools such as choppers for cutting, knives for skinning, and scrapers for processing hides. Most of the Paleo-Indian sites are located in Southern Michigan along the lake side. However, an extraordinary collection of over 20 spear points were excavated near Deer Lake in Marquette County in 1987, dating back to 7500 BCE, proving that these ancient people also occupied the Upper Peninsula.

MINING COPPER

Perhaps the most astonishing discovery concerning these early inhabitants is the existence of copper mines on Isle Royale and the Keewenaw Peninsula, dating to around 5000 BCE. Using wooden and stone tools, these Copper Culture people dug small pits to get at the native copper lying very near the surface. Some of these pits are up to 80 feet deep, and in these two locations there are 5,000 pits, suggesting a major industry. The people extracted the copper from between layers of solid rock using fire and cold water. They then heated the metal and threw water at the hot rock, cracking it. They pounded the copper pieces into flat sheets, folded, heated, and cooled the sheets to toughen them, then pounded, refolded, and hammered them again to produce both useful and decorative items. Great Lakes natives produced remarkable heavy copper tools along with knives, spear points, fish hooks, axes, and needles. They were among the first people on earth to make metal tools.

They also made decorative items such as bracelets and other jewelry. The discovery of Michigan copper items in places as far west as North Dakota and as far east as Quebec suggest a lucrative trade was taking place.

Some speculate that these Copper Culture people traded with the Phoenicians and the Vikings. The latter left their mark near present-day Toronto, indicating with petroglyphs and writings that their trading mission was well-established in copper in the year 1700 BCE.

THE MOUND BUILDERS

Another group of prehistoric people known to have occupied Michigan were the Hopewell Indians. They take their name from the farmer on whose land their burial mound was found in Ohio. Their primary centers were in the central Mississippi, Ohio, and Illinois river valleys dating back to 500 BCE. They were farmers, traders, and artists of exceptional talent who buried their dead under mounds of soil.

About 100 BCE, some of the Hopewells entered the Great Lakes region from Illinois, traveling by water and settling in the St. Joseph River Valley in southwestern Michigan. After establishing settlements along the upper Kankakee and lower St. Joseph rivers, they moved into western Michigan, first to the Kalamazoo Valley, then to the lower Grand River Valley, where they established an important ceremonial center near the present-day site of Grand Rapids. Groups of these Hopewells later moved north into the Muskegon River Valley, the farthest north they settled.

Quite a lot is known of these inhabitants from studying the contents of their burial mounds. They hunted all of the available animals, especially deer, and had dogs as their sole domesticated animal. They were of medium height and stocky, with oval faces and "slant" eyes. The men wore breechcloths of skin while the women wore wrap-around skirts of woven cloth or skin. The Hopewells made great use of non-indigenous raw materials for the manufacture of everyday implements, obtaining obsidian from the Rocky Mountains for blades and grizzly bear teeth for ornaments. Large sea shells came from the south Atlantic coast and the Gulf of Mexico. They brought in lead from Missouri and Illinois and copper and silver from the north. From the

The Petoskey Stone

During the Devonian Period some 350 million years ago, Michigan was near the equator. Coral reefs grew in the warm shallow seas that covered the area, and when buried the corals were fossilized. A genuine Petoskey stone is a type of hexagonal coral with honeycomb cells that are revealed when the stone is polished. It is found in limestone formations near Petoskey, near the northern tip of the Lower Peninsula. The glaciers gouged the stones from the bedrock and spread them across the state. The Petoskey Stone was made Michigan's state stone in 1965.

middle Atlantic coast, they also obtained sheets of mica, all of which point to a widespread commerce.

The Hopewell culture flourished from about 100 BCE to 700 CE, when they faded from the scene. Their culture in Michigan represented a climax or a sort of classical period, if you will, the like of which was never achieved again.

Other peoples were living in the upper Great Lakes region at the same time as the Hopewells. These neighbors had a much simpler culture. Some of them made their living by farming and fishing and others only by hunting and fishing. The archeological record for these groups is less reliable than for the Hopewells, but what has been found is reflective of their culture, albeit on a much simpler scale. These native groups would evolve into the people that the Europeans would encounter beginning in the 1600s.

ANISHNABEG

The people living in the upper Great Lakes region at the beginning of the historic period (generally accepted as 1600 CE) would—had one had the chance to ask them—have identified themselves as Anishnabeg instead of as a member of a specific tribe. This term would indicate that they were Algonquin speakers, sharing that identity with their neighbors who spoke the same—or nearly the same—language. These people would also have shared the same customs and traditions. Among those common beliefs was that the Anishnabeg were the "true" people, the descendants of the people of their mythology. Beyond this, they would have made reference to belonging to a kin group or clan.

There are three clans most commonly associated with Michigan and who were present when the first Europeans arrived: the Ojibwa (Chippewa); the Odawa (Ottawa); and the Potawatomie. Together these three tribes formed the Three Fires Confederacy, a loose-knit alliance that promoted mutual interests.

The Ojibwa, the largest of these groups, lived mostly in the Upper Peninsula and along the northern shore of Lake Superior and Georgian Bay. They numbered between 25,000 to 35,000 among their various bands. Some 4,000 Potawatomi occupied the western half of the Lower Peninsula and approximately 3,500 Odawa lived in the eastern half and along the eastern shore of Georgian Bay.

There were other tribes living in the upper Great Lakes region as well. Along the western shore of Lake Michigan, in present-day Wisconsin, were the Winnebago, Menominee, Sauk, and Fox; in northern Indiana and Illinois were the Miami tribe; and along the eastern shore of Lake Huron lived the largest of the area's tribes, some 45,000 to 60,000 of the Huron.

The Huron were members of the Iroquois Confederation and spoke a different language than the other inhabitants of the region. They moved from their homeland to Ontario after becoming enemies of the Iroquois and lived between Lake Simcoe and Georgian Bay and west of Lake Simcoe to Lake Huron. They lived in towns and villages, some of which were protected by circular palisades 15 to 35 feet high made of upright logs complete with watchtowers. One of the largest towns contained 200 large houses in which 4,000 to 6,000 people lived.

These houses were quite sophisticated, being 150 to 180 feet long, 36 feet wide and 24 feet high. They were made of poles eight feet thick and covered with slabs of bark. Around the interior wall were sleeping platforms four feet high covered with woven mats. Each house was divided into compartments for individual families sharing five fires. The Huron were basically farmers who supplemented their diets by hunting and fishing. It was among these people that the first Europeans to the Great Lakes area made contact.

THE PASSAGE TO THE ORIENT

By the beginning of the 17th century, sailing ships from many different countries of the Old World were visiting the coasts of the New on a very regular basis. Crews of French, Spanish, Portuguese, Dutch, and English ships fished, hunted whales, captured natives for slaves and, on occasion, traded for furs from the Hudson Straits to Florida.

Following the route taken by Jacques Cartier, French explorer Samuel Champlain pushed up the St. Lawrence River to establish Quebec in 1608. In part to find a shorter route to China, the French began to explore the Great Lakes region and soon established a relationship with the Algonquin speaking people who occupied the valley and the country to the west and north.

Arriving with Champlain was a 16-year-old named Etienne (Stephen) Brule who was to play an important role in Michigan history. He was one of several young men of intelligence that Champlain placed with a few friendly tribes to spend the winter (non-trading season) and learn the language and the surrounding country. In addition to gathering intelligence, this procedure did much to cement good relations with the tribes.

The natives who traded at Montreal regaled Champlain with stories of the western country that included mention of great seas to the north and west. Thinking that he had discovered a route to the Orient but finding no one who would guide him there, Champlain settled on sending Brule with the Hurons to winter in the west. The lad was anxious to go in 1610 he left Quebec and became the first white man to travel the route later followed by the voyageurs and touch the shores of Lake Nipissing, Georgian Bay, and Lake Huron. Brule's crowning achievement was the discovery of Lake Superior in 1622.

By 1634, Champlain had established more or less permanent settlements at Quebec and Montreal on the St. Lawrence, and a thriving fur trade was an annual event at the latter post. He decided to make one more attempt to locate a passage to the Orient. Fur company agent and interpreter Jean Nicholet was sent west along the Ottawa River route to find such a passage. He was provided with an elaborate Chinese robe to wear when he met them. Nicholet traveled through the Straits of Mackinac and along the north shore of

Lake Michigan until he came to Green Bay, Wisconsin. Thinking he had found the way to Cathay, Nicholet disembarked dressed in his robe and managed to impress some 4,000 or 5,000 Winnebago and Menominee natives. Realizing that he was not anywhere near China, Nicholet fired off some guns and laid claim to the land for France.

MISSIONARIES AND EXPLORERS

Shortly after Nicholet's expedition through the upper lakes, the mission to Christianize the natives began in earnest. Members of the Society of Jesus, the Jesuits, were zealous missionaries bent on bringing God's light to the heathens.

Jean de Brebeuf was the first Jesuit to enter the Huron country along Georgian Bay and the first to die for his faith. He first went to the Huron in 1625, accompanied by two other priests. Four years later, the defeat of the French by the English caused all priests to be withdrawn from Canada. A treaty between the two belligerents in 1632 restored the country to France and the Jesuits built a fortified mission named Ste. Marie in Ontario, Canada.

In 1641 Fathers Isaac Jogues and Charles Raymbault set out from there by canoe north to the St. Mary's River between the Upper Peninsula and Canada. Near the Rapids they found an native village of 2,000 souls and said a mass, probably the first in Michigan, at that place which they named Sault Ste. Marie, "sault" meaning rapids. Their mission was a temporary one and they returned to their headquarters in Canada. Other missionaries would soon follow with varying degrees of success. In 1660 Father Rene Menard traveled to the western end of Lake Superior to minister to some Hurons who had fled there after an attack by the Iroquois. He followed the southern shore of the lake until he came to Keweenaw Bay. Menard spent the winter with an Ottawa tribe and the following spring headed farther west and was never seen or heard from again. Another, Father Claude Allonez, reported that he found copper in the Keweenaw and repeated stories that he had heard about a great river which lay to the west of Lake Superior, a river that was actually the Mississippi.

One of the best known Jesuit missionaries made his way to Michigan in 1668. Father Jacques Marquette arrived at Sault Ste. Marie with instructions to establish a

permanent mission there. From this post, Michigan's oldest city developed. The following spring he was sent to Chequamegon Bay in Wisconsin. While there he heard from visiting Illinois natives of the great river Mississippi. The Huron and Odawa at this mission, who had fled from the Iroquois, soon had another enemy. Some Sioux were murdered and, rather than face destruction at the hands of these western natives, they fled eastward along the Michigan shore of Lake Superior, then south to the Straits of Mackinac. Marquette had no choice but to follow his parishioners. In the summer of 1671, he established another mission and named it St. Ignace, after the founder of the Jesuits, Ignatius Loyola. The natives called the region around the Straits, including Mackinac Island, Michilimackinac, and this crossroads of the lakes would become an important stopping place for missionaries,

Lake Michigan
Photodisc Green/Getty Images

traders, and the king's officers as well as every tribe that used the Great Lakes.

Up until the year 1669, there is no record of a white man ever visiting the Lower Peninsula of Michigan, although it is very likely that some "coureurs de bois," or voyageurs, did and left no record of it. The French were confined to the slower northern route from Montreal to Georgian Bay because of conflict with the Iroquois, who controlled the southern route through Lakes Ontario and Erie. This situation changed for a time during the late 1600s after King Louis XIV sent out an army regiment, who defeated the Iroquois in 1667 and opened up the lower lake route.

The first white man to take this route was Louis Jolliet, a veteran trader and explorer who was at Sault Ste. Marie preparing to return to Quebec after an unsuccessful search for an Upper Peninsula copper mine. An Iroquois prisoner released by the terms of the recent treaty offered to guide him back through the lower lakes.

Jolliet accepted the offer and they paddled their canoe along the Michigan shore of Lake Huron through the St. Clair River, Lake St. Clair, the Detroit River, and the north shore of Lake Erie. They traveled overland from Lake Erie to the western end of Lake Ontario.

Near present-day Hamilton, Ontario, they ran into a party of Frenchmen and natives headed west, led by Robert Cavelier, Sieur de la Salle. La Salle had set out from Quebec to discover the Ohio River accompanied by two Sulpician priests eager to establish a mission among the distant tribes.

Jolliet drew them a map of the route he had just taken and urged them to take it to the north country where there were plenty of souls to save. La Salle would not be deterred from his purpose, but the two priests, Fathers Francois Dollier and Rene Galinee, were enthusiastic enough to go it alone. They wintered along the north shore of Erie and in the spring of 1670 set out for the Upper Lakes. Galinee kept a journal, which contains the first description of the Detroit River, Lake St. Clair, and the St. Clair River.

After spending a night at Point Pelee and losing some supplies and their altar service to an overnight storm, Galinee writes:

> We pursued our journey accordingly toward the west and after making about 100 leagues on Lake Erie, arrived at the place where the Lake of the Hurons, otherwise called the "Freshwater Sea" of the Hurons, or Michigan, discharges into this Lake. This outlet is perhaps half a league in width and turns sharp to the northeast, so that we were almost retracing our path. At the end of six leagues, we discovered a place that is very remarkable and held in great veneration by all the Indians of these countries because of a stone idol that nature had formed there. To it they say they owe their good luck in sailing on Lake Erie, when they cross it without accident and they propitiate it by sacrifices, presents of skins, provisions, etc., when they wish to

Sanilac Petroglyphs

Near Cass City and Bad Axe, mythical water panthers, deer, and a Native American archer roam the banks of the north branch of the Cass River. Etched into an outcrop of sandstone by unknown prehistoric artists, these massive carvings were first discovered after huge forest fires swept the Lower Peninsula clear of trees in 1881. Native Americans created this unusual artwork 300 to 1000 years ago, giving a glimpse into the lives of ancient woodland people who once occupied the thumb area of Michigan. A self-guided nature trail winding through the woods and across the Cass River provides an opportunity to see the past.

embark on it. The place was full of camps of those who had come to pay their homage to this stone, which had no other resemblance to the figure of a man than what the imagination was pleased to give it. However, it was all painted and a sort of face had been formed for it with vermilion. I eave to imagine whether we avenged upon this idol, which the Iroquois had strongly recommended us to honor, the loss of our chapel. We attributed to it even the dearth of provisions from which we had hitherto suffered. In short, there was nobody whose hatred it had not incurred. I consecrated one of my axes to break this god of stone and then, having yoked our canoes together, we carried the largest piece to the middle of the river and threw all the rest also into the water, in order that it might never be heard of again. God rewarded us immediately for this good action, for we killed a roe buck [and a bear] that very day. At the end of four leagues we entered a small lake [St. Clair], about ten leagues in length and almost as many in width, called by Mr. Sanson [a Paris mapmaker], The Salt Water Lake, but we saw no sign of salt in this lake.

Louis Jolliet, the son of a wagon maker, was born in Quebec in 1645, making him the first noteworthy man of European descent to be born on North American soil. A veteran explorer of the Great Lakes region, Jolliet was given the task in 1672 of exploring the "grand river"

The A.E. Seaman Museum

The A.E. Seaman Museum, established in 1902, houses one of the top crystal collections in North America and showcases the world's finest displays of minerals from Michigan's Lake Superior Copper District. Located on the campus of Michigan Technological University in Houghton, Michigan, the museum was designated the official Mineralogical Museum of Michigan by the State Legislature in 1990.

beyond the lakes, which the natives claimed flowed into the southern sea. He also carried orders for Marquette to accompany him. In May, 1673, with five voyageurs and two canoes, they began their journey. By June, they reached the Fox River and a short portage found them on the Wisconsin River. On June 17, the party paddled into the waters of the Mississippi. On the return trip Marquette fell ill and was forced to stay at Green Bay until the fall of 1674. Enroute home to St. Ignace, he died and was buried near present-day Ludington. He was 38 years old.

The discovery of the headwaters of the Mississippi proved the native tales true. But into what sea did it flow? This question would be answered by La Salle, who may or may not have discovered the Ohio River. It was his plan to explore the river to its mouth and erect a chain of forts that would prevent the English from settling in the middle of the continent. He would also carry on the fur trade, proceeds from which would have to pay for the expedition, as no funds were forthcoming from King Louis XIV.

To provide transportation for the large amount of furs La Salle expected to gather in the west, he had a little sailing vessel built on the bank of the Niagara River above the Falls. At the prow he had carved the figure of a griffon, a mythical beast with the body of a lion and the head of an eagle, taken from the coat of arms of his patron, Count Frontenac. The ship mounted five small cannon and was named after the figurehead. The *Griffon* was the first sailing vessel on the Great Lakes.

In August, 1679, La Salle and his crew of 30 sailed

westward across Lake Erie. A Recollet priest accompanied them, and Father Louis Hennepin kept a journal from where we get one of the first written descriptions of the Lower Peninsula:

> We reached the entrance of the Detroit [strait] by which Lake Orleans [Huron] empties into Lake Conty [Erie].... This strait is thirty leagues long and almost everywhere a league wide, except in the middle where it expands and forms a lake of circular form, which we called Lake St. Claire, on account of our passing through it on that Saint's day.
>
> The country on both sides of this beautiful strait is adorned with fine open plains and you can see numbers of stags, does, deer, bears, by no means fierce and very good to eat.... The rest of the strait is covered with forests, fruit trees, like walnuts, chestnuts, plums and apple trees, wild vines loaded with grapes, of which we made some little wine. There is timber fit for building. It is a place in which deer most delight.

Upon entering Lake Huron, the ship was beset by a severe storm which it managed to weather and La Salle coasted into St. Ignace. After resting several days, they set sail for the entrance of Green Bay, Wisconsin, where they picked up a large cargo of furs. La Salle, who according to Hennepin never took anyone's advice, decided to send the loaded ship back to Niagara and continue his voyage by canoe. To this day, that was the last that anyone has seen of the *Griffon*. La Salle and his men continued on their way

Norton Mounds

The Norton Mound group is one of the most significant Hopwellian burial centers in the country and one of the most important archaeological sites in Michigan. First excavated in 1874, the site consisted of 17 mounds ranging from 30 feet in diameter to 100 feet. Once part of a system of over 30 mounds, 11 remain in their basic form. The site represents a fine example of the northern extension of the Hopewell culture.

Stephen Brule (1592-1633)

Stephen Brule left his home in France and set sail for the new colony of Quebec at the age of 16. Champlain sent him to live among the Huron people in 1610, where he learned their language and customs. He was an excellent scout and pathfinder who went on many expeditions for Champlain and the fur traders. Brule later left the colony and lived with the Huron for over 20 years and became a great disappointment to Champlain, who believed that Brule led the British to the capture of Quebec in 1629. The truth of this allegation may never be known as the Huron killed Brule a few years later. Champlain's reply to the news was that he would not seek justice for the murder of a traitor.

along the west coast of Lake Michigan in four large canoes. They continued around the southern end of the lake to the mouth of the St. Joseph River, where in November 1679 La Salle built Fort Miami on the present-day site of St. Joseph, Michigan. He made one trip into the Illinois country that winter and returned to Fort Miami where he waited in desperation for the return of the *Griffon*. Early in the spring of 1680, discouraged and short of supplies, La Salle and his men set out to return to Fort Frontenac. Reasoning that the most direct route would be to cross Michigan's Lower Peninsula, they walked from Fort Miami to the Detroit area, their only provisions the game they could kill. The exact route is not known, but they probably passed through the second tier of counties above the Indiana–Ohio borders until they struck the Huron River near Ann Arbor and followed it to Lake Erie. Two years later, La Salle would sail down the Mississippi to its mouth, claiming most of the middle of North America for France. His explorations were helpful in gaining knowledge of more of the Great Lakes region and the western fur trade.

Another great explorer who spent some time in Michigan was a man by the name of Daniel Greysolon, Sieur Duluth, who traded furs on a large scale. On numerous occasions, he was at the Sault or St. Ignace and was able to make peace between the Michigan tribes and the Sioux, thereby opening the West beyond Lake Superior to the French. In 1686 the Governor of New France, Denonville, ordered Duluth to build a fort between Lakes Huron and Erie to prevent English traders from reaching the Upper Lakes. The previous year, an English merchant named Roseboom reached Michilimackinac with 11 canoes filled with cheaper trade goods. He promised an eager native clientele to return the following season. Duluth left Michilimacknac with 50 coureur de bois and chose a spot at the head of the St. Clair River, now present-day Port Huron, to build his stockade. The post would remain in existence for only the next two years before being burned and abandoned.

Two other French establishments came into existence at this time. One was at Michilimackinac on the St. Ignace side of the Strait and the other was 25 miles upriver from La Salle's Fort Miami and named Fort St. Joseph, near the present-day site of Niles, Michigan. Augustin de Gardeur, Sieur de Courtemanche was appointed commandant at this post and in 1694 successfully defended it against a large party of Iroquois. In that same year, Frontenac appointed a new commander at Fort de Buude, a man he praised for his valor, wisdom, experience, and good conduct. His name was Antoine de la Mothe Cadillac and his appointment gave him supervision over all of the other posts in the West. He soon became embroiled with the Jesuits over the sale of brandy to the Native Americans, the beginning of a feud that would have disastrous consequences for him.

Lake Transportation

Transportation on the Great Lakes was primarily by birch bark canoe, most commonly associated with the Native Americans of the northern New England regions. They were of all sizes, made small for a single person or large enough to carry 50 paddlers. They ranged in length from 10 to 40 feet. The canoes were lightweight yet strong enough to carry up to 4 tons of goods. Made of bark from the white birch, strips of which had to be removed from the tree according to the size of the canoe as the bark was not pieced together, these vessels served as temporary shelters enroute by being upturned and supported by a stout stick.

2

De'Troit

The explorations that opened up the Great Lakes region west of Lake Superior to the fur trade flooded the European market for those furs and caused King Louis XIV in 1696 to order the withdrawal of all French traders, soldiers, and settlers from the "west," which included the Michigan area. Prices for furs were dropping rapidly and businessmen could not continue to make a profit unless the supply was cut back. This royal decree would also mollify the Jesuits, who were up in arms over the traders' habit of supplying alcohol to the native tribes.

Antoine Cadillac abandoned Fort de Baude in 1698. He had made a great deal of money at Michilimackinac in the fur trade and had been able to hold the Native Americans in alliance with France. He had also written an extensive "Memoir" of his three years in command, which gives us an excellent picture of the lake region with much information of the country and details of native life and customs. But for a man with Cadillac's ambition, these achievements were not enough. When he arrived at Quebec in the early fall of 1698, he had a plan which he presented to Frontenac, who approved it and sent Cadillac back to France with a letter of recommendation to the king.

Cadillac sought to obtain permission to establish a permanent settlement at some point on the strait (de'troit) between Lake St. Clair and Lake Erie. It would cost the king nothing to build and maintain, all expenses to be paid from the profits of the fur trade. Cadillac would also ask King Louis to grant him a *seigniory* which would entitle him to make land grants to settlers. In the face of the king's recent order closing all posts, his major selling point would be to call the king's attention to the growing danger from the British, the subsequent loss of the fur trade for good, and the strategic position of a fort on the strait, much superior to Michilimackinac.

In Paris, Cadillac convinced Louis Phelypeaux, Count Ponchartrain, the Minister of Marine, of the need for such a fort. An audience with Louis XIV got him the necessary orders to the governor of New France to assist him in carrying out his plans. When Cadillac returned to Quebec, he discovered that his patron, Frontenac, had died shortly after he had sailed for France. His successor, Governor Callieres, did not like Cadillac but had no choice than to obey an order from the king.

Hostilities with the Iroquois in 1701 closed the faster southern lake route from Quebec to Michigan to the French, so Cadillac had to take the longer, northern route. On June 5, 1701, he set out from Montreal with 100 French-Canadians and 100 Algonquin in 25 large canoes to establish a new settlement along the lower Great Lakes. With Cadillac was his eight-year-old son Antoine, his second-in-command Alphonse de Tonty, two lieutenants, two priests, 50 soldiers, and 50 voyageurs and settlers. From Montreal, the group paddled up the Ottawa River across to Lake Nipissing, then across the lake and down the French and Pickerel Rivers to Georgian Bay and across the bay to Lake Huron. Following the eastern shoreline, the flotilla moved through Lake St. Clair and down the Detroit River to Grosse Isle. Toward dusk on July 23, they made camp on Grosse Isle after a trip of 600 miles and 30 portages—in all, an arduous journey.

Deciding not to stay on the island mostly because of a lack of wood, they paddled the following morning back upriver to search out the best possible site for a fortified town. Cadillac saw that a bluff almost 40 feet high faced the narrowest point of the river on each side. With a solder's eye, he noted that the bluff on the western side ended abruptly in a small hill and around the foot of the hill ran a small river or stream that emptied into the Detroit. With the best defensive position chosen, the French party landed, climbed the bluff, and claimed the land in the name of King Louis XIV.

After a brief prayer of thanks for a safe arrival, the group started clearing a plot of land, felling trees for the stockade fence and housing. The trees cut for the fence were six to eight inches in diameter and 12 to 15 feet in length. They were set in a trench dug about four feet deep. The fort would eventually occupy a square arpent of

Fort Ponchartrain du Detroit

The fort's walls enclosed one square arpent of land as Cadillac marked it out. The southern border was present-day Jefferson Avenue; the northern border was between present-day Larned Street and Jefferson; the eastern end was approximately where Griswold Street is today; and the western end was along present-day Shelby Street. There were at least two gates built in the palisades, one along the southern side by the river and the other on the east side by St. Anne's Church. There were at most five streets inside the palisade: St. Anne, running east to west; St. Joachim, running parallel to St. Anne; St. Francois and St. Antoine, running in a north-south direction; and a small street, really nothing but an alley, named Recontre.

land—192.75 feet on each side, or nearly one acre. A deep ditch was dug along each outside wall to improve the fort's defenses. The walls went up rather quickly and, although no record of the amount of work completed each day exists, it is known that the first building erected within the fort was the church, named on July 26, 1701, St. Anne's day, two days after landing.

The houses were constructed by setting logs on end in a trench. Each house was one story high, with walls just over six feet tall and roofed with thatch. Other buildings erected (all belonging to Cadillac) were a warehouse constructed with plank, which held a counter and a press for boiling skins and a door fitted with lock and key; another building, about 19 by 33 feet, also had a locking door. Additional constructions included a smaller building, 12 by 18 by 6.5 feet high; a barn for storing crops; another building constructed of split stakes and without a door; an ice house 15 feet square, six feet high above ground and 15 feet beneath the surface; and one last building of inferior build.

By September 1, 1701, the enclosure was complete. Cadillac named the fort in honor of his patron at court, Count Ponchartrain. It was known as Fort Ponchartrain du Detroit, later shortened to simply Detroit.

Sunrise over Lake Huron near Presque Isle. Vito Palmisano

In a letter dated October 5, 1701, Cadillac described the land surrounding the fort:

> The banks are so vast many meadows where the freshness of three beautiful streams keep the grass always green. These same meadows are fringed with long and broad avenues of fruit trees, young and old, [which] droop down under the weight and multitude of their fruit. In this soil so fertile, the ambitious vine forms a thick roof with its heavy clusters over the head of whatever it twines around. Under these vast avenues you may see assembling in hundreds, the shy stag and the timid hind with the bounding roebuck, to pick up eagerly the apples and plums with which the ground is paved. It is there that the turkey hen calls back her numerous brood and leads them to gather the grapes. The golden pheasant, the quail, the partridge, the woodcock, the teeming turtledove swarm in the woods and cover the open country intersected and broken by groves of full-grown forest trees.
>
> The woods are of six kinds—walnut, white oaks, red, ash, ivy, white wood trees and cottonwood trees.

They are as straight as arrows, without knots and almost without branches except near the top. It is from these branches that the fearless eagle looks steadily at the sun.

The fish there are fed and laved in sparkling and pellucid waters. There are such large numbers of swans that the rushes among which they are massed might be taken for lilies. The gabbling goose, the duck, the teal and the bustard are so common there that they only move aside long enough to allow the boat to pass.

Cadillac's plan for establishing a new post included the Native Americans living around or near the fort. By late fall, as many as 6,000 lived in the vicinity of the post. A Huron village below the fort and a larger village containing four tribes of Ottawas above the fort were set up on land granted to them by the commandant. Even though the tribes could get a better price for their furs from the English at Hudson's Bay, they preferred to trade with the French, who were more in tune with their way of life. As word of the new settlement spread, more of them came to Detroit to trade.

In order to quell rumors that Fort Ponchartrain was only a temporary post, Cadillac sent word for his wife and Madame de Tonty to join them. In the fall of 1701, the two ladies along with six-year-old Jacque Cadillac set out by canoe from Montreal. Accompanied by some Native American guides and rough voyageurs, they traveled the lower lakes route, as a treaty had been settled with the Iroquois shortly after Cadillac left Quebec. The first white women to live in Michigan arrived in the spring of 1702, amid much fanfare. The Iroquois were impressed that the French women made the trip from Quebec.

About their reaction, Cadillac wrote:

It is certain that nothing [even] astonished the Iroquois as greatly as when they saw them. You could not believe how many caresses they offered them, and particularly the Iroquois, who kissed their hands and wept for joy, saying that French women had never been seen coming willingly to their country. It was that which made the Iroquois also say that they well knew that the general peace... was indeed sincere, and that they could no longer doubt it since women of this rank came amongst them with so much confidence.

For the next four years, Detroit remained at peace with the Native Americans. The settlement continued to grow, but slowly. Cadillac was not an easy man for settlers to work with, as he charged high prices and was cold-hearted in his business dealings. He had many enemies throughout New France, especially among the Montreal merchants and the Jesuits, and the people were not above spreading rumors and lies about the new settlement. The fact that the French were not as interested in settling down and building towns or farms as the British colonists only added to their problems.

Besides being commandant of the fort and having the trade monopoly, Cadillac also wanted to be the "seignor" of the region, or the feudal landowner. He would owe homage to the king and be his vassal. In return Cadillac would be able to grant land to tenants, build a mill for their use, perform military service, and be the judge in his seigniory.

On June 14, 1704, Count Ponchartrain wrote to Cadillac advising him of a decree giving him the authority to make conveyances of land and collect rent, although he was not granted a seigniory. Cadillac made approximately 150 grants of land between 1707 and 1710, and they were divided as follows: 68 city lots; 31 farms; and 13 gardens. One of these early grants was to Marie LePage, the only record of a conveyance to a woman in early Detroit. Marie was the wife of Francois Beauceron, two of a large influx of 58 settlers who arrived in Detroit in 1706. In that year, Paul and Jean Lescuyer brought 10 head of cattle and three horns to Detroit. These were the first domestic animals in the West.

RIBBON FARMS

The city lots granted by Cadillac were all within the stockade walls and not very big, on average 20 by 25 feet in size. The farm lots were quite unusual in size and function and similar to those that were granted along the St. Lawrence River. As there were no roads yet, the river was the fastest transportation system available and every family had a canoe. Hence, every farm had access to the river. These farms were about 250 feet wide and one and one half to three miles deep, the longest extending from the river to what is now Harper Avenue. The abundance of game and fruit, a successful wheat crop sown by Cadillac in 1701, and the fact that the early settlers were soldiers or traders kept agricultural development to a minimum. Cadillac allowed every resident to participate in the fur trade in exchange for an annual fee of five livres, not an unobtainable amount of money.

THE FUR TRADE

The animals of North America produced the finest furs in the world. The climate of the northern sections was adapted to the growth of these animals in almost perfect conditions. Beaver, silver fox, red fox, wolverine, fisher, mink, otter, lynx, black bear, and others were found in abundance across the state and the Great Lakes region. The furs had a ready market virtually anywhere in the world and were easily obtained from the Native Americans. The struggle for control over this $100 million-plus industry began between France and England in the late 1600s and ended with France's surrender of its entire North American empire in 1763.

Men of influence and wealth formed companies to exploit and control the trade, earning enormous fortunes and influence over extensive territories in the process. In the beginning, it was the wood rangers, or *coureur de bois*, who went directly to the Native Americans to trade for furs. These men were a hardy lot with little or no ties to the old country and family. Assimilating themselves into the native culture and becoming more native than white, often taking Native American wives, they did as much to bring the trade to the French as any post commandant or trading company did.

Their favorite trading rendezvous were Sault Ste. Marie and Michilimackinac. The opening of the post at Detroit did everything to close both of those locations as large, active trading centers. The Ottawa and Huron, Miami and Chippewa all accepted Cadillac's invitation to establish their villages above and below Detroit. So many Native Americans left Michilimackinac that Father Carmel burned the chapel at St. Ignace in 1705 and returned to Quebec. Some coureur de bois still used the upper sites but not to any great extent. The fur trade at this point was centered at Detroit.

No sooner had Cadillac left Montreal on his trip to establish the new post than the trade monopoly granted to him was taken away and given instead to a group named the Company of the Colony. This was accomplished through subterfuge at court in Versailles and with the collusion of the

governor-general of New France. Cadillac returned several times to Quebec to attempt to get the agreement changed, but to no avail. In 1705, he was arrested in Quebec and placed on trial for misdeeds in the fur trade, mainly theft and mismanagement. Both the Jesuits and Montreal merchants had a hand in these so-called charges. Cadillac was acquitted but did not return to Detroit until August, 1706. In his absence, Lieutenant Sieur de Bourgmont, in temporary command, sided with the Miami tribe in their quarrel with the Ottawa. In revenge, the Ottawa killed a French soldier and fled the fort, stopping just long enough to catch Father Del le Halle in his garden outside the stockade fence and kill him. The Recollet priest became the first civilian victim of violence in Detroit. Bourgmont then ordered his soldiers to fire at the Ottawa, killing about 30 of them. Cadillac returned in time to prevent further mayhem. With his acquittal, he had regained total control over Detroit and the fur trade.

MICHILIMACKINAC

In 1708 Francois Clarembault, Sieur d'Aigremont, arrived in Detroit and stayed 19 days. Aigremont was a sub-delegate of the Surveyor and the King's Deputy for surveying all of the military posts in Canada. His report on the conditions at Detroit was not complimentary toward Cadillac and replete with petty charges against him. The settlement at Detroit had grown but slowly since its founding and several structures were in need of repair. This report also contained the recommendation that a new post be established at Michimackinac in order to regulate the fur trade. Acting on this recommendation, the French erected a new fort at the Straits in 1710 on the south side at the tip of the lower Peninsula.

CADILLAC OUSTED

Shortly after the birth of his son, Francois, on March 27, 1709, Cadillac received a letter from his patron at court, Count Ponchartrain, complaining that the commander

Augusta covered bridge over Augusta Creek located in Kalamazoo County
David Vaughn

shows "too much greed" and "too little moderation" in his dealings with the settlers at Detroit. Cadillac's enemies at court in Paris and Quebec were increasing the pressure on the government to have him relieved of his command, if not imprisoned and executed. Finally, in 1710, the French government relieved him of his post and named him governor of the new colony of Louisiana, with headquarters on Mobile Bay. Although it was a promotion, the move to Louisiana proved to be a financial disaster for the Cadillac family, as they had to leave nearly everything they owned in Detroit. The family would never be fully reimbursed for their lost possessions. Cadillac delayed his departure until August of 1711, when he left Detroit, never to return.

NATIVE TROUBLES

No sooner had Cadillac departed for Louisiana than a party of about 1,000 Fox natives arrived at Detroit and asked to see him. Several years earlier he had invited them to settle at the Strait from their home in Wisconsin. Disappointed to learn that Cadillac had left, Dubisson could do nothing but watch and wait while the newcomers under their chief, Lalima, fortified their camp and killed what animals they found for food. They also insulted the resident Huron and Ottawa men and women, threatening to murder them all.

Dubisson immediately dispatched messengers to the winter camps of his Native American allies, pleading for assistance. Most of the fort's supplies were outside of the palisade and an order was issued to bring in as much corn and other foodstuffs as they could. A detail of soldiers was ordered to level all of the buildings that were near enough to the fort to provide cover for the Fox marksmen. St. Anne's Church was one of the buildings torn down. As the settlers retreated into the fort, the Fox began their attack.

Luckily, help was on the way. On May 13, Jean-Baptiste Bissot, Sieur de Vincennes, arrived from the Miami country with seven French traders. Surprising the Fox, they ran through their lines and reached the fort with no casualties. Shortly after that, word came from the Huron camp that their warriors and the Ottawa had arrived from their winter camp. Vincennes sortied from the fort to confirm this news and reported to Dubisson that the Native Americans were determined to exterminate the Fox. The tide was starting to turn and the besiegers were becoming the besieged. Because Lalima and his followers had taken some of the garrison's provisions, they could withstand a short siege. Their only problem was a shortage of water, as they had not bothered to dig wells.

Iaguima, the Ottawa war chief, received powder and shot from the French and with the soldiers on the stockade walls began an intermittent fire on the Fox camp. To escape this nuisance, the Fox warriors dug pits four or five feet deep to conceal themselves. Dubisson ordered his men to erect scaffolds in the fort high enough for them to shoot into the pits. This forced the Fox to abandon the pits under cover of darkness and find a safer position.

Daylight found the Fox in possession of a house within easy gunshot range of the fort. Their best marksmen were stationed on the roof and began to pour fire into the fort. Dubisson ordered a small swivel gun hoisted to the top of one of the scaffolds and the second shot cleared the roof of snipers, killing several of them.

After several days of this fighting, the Fox began a taunting discussion with one of the Pottawotomie chiefs. While everyone was watching this discourse, several of the Fox women made their way to the river for water. Dubisson saw their movements, and hostilities re-commenced. A separate band of Mascouten attempted to relieve or reinforce the Fox, but they were captured by the Ottawa and carried to Detroit, where they were systematically tortured and killed within sight of the Fox camp.

The next day, Lalima attempted to obtain a truce with the French. In exchange for three Ottawa women that he held hostage, he asked permission to leave Detroit and return unmolested to Wisconsin. After surrendering the women, Dubisson denounced the Fox as "dogs" and ordered them back to their camp so that the conflict could resume. Incensed by the betrayal, the Fox fought back with a vengeance, launching hundreds of fire arrows at Fort Ponchartrain, setting fire to the thatched roofs of the barracks and to the storehouses containing foodstuffs and furs. The fort's defenders were prepared and, using two canoes filled with water, succeeded in extinguishing the flames without losing too many materials. The morale on both sides was beginning to deteriorate after two weeks of fighting.

In the Fox fortified camp, conditions had become desperate. Chronically short of water, the Fox made separate sorties toward the Detroit River. Each attempt was defeated by the Ottawa with considerable loss of life. By the last week in May, their food supplies were nearly gone, and since the French continued to fire into their camp they were also unable to bury the dead. The decomposing bodies created an environment ripe for disease, and weakened by malnutrition almost 70 women and children perished. Still they fought on, returning enough firepower to keep their enemies from storming their fortifications.

On the evening of the 19th day of the siege, May 30, 1712, nature intervened. A long line of spring thunderstorms spread across southern Michigan from the west. The Detroit area was inundated with rain and the besiegers took shelter in the fort or the Huron village. The Fox and remaining Mascoutens hastily packed what was left of the ammunition and at around midnight abandoned their camp. They headed northeast, under the cover of the

St. Anne's Church

The first building to be erected after the stockade fence, St. Anne's is the second oldest Catholic parish in the United States, established on July 26, 1701. This building was destroyed by a fire in 1703 and consumed the earliest parish records. The present building that is the church was erected in 1886 and is the eighth named for St. Anne. Located near the Ambassador Bridge, it is a gothic style church with flying buttresses prominent on the exterior. The church contains many relics from the 1818 stone church, including the main altar, the hand-carved communion rail, and the oldest stained glass in the city. It also houses the coffin of its most famous pastor, Father Gabriel Richard.

storm, following the Detroit River and hoping to secure some canoes to cross over into Canada. The Grosse Pointe area, soon to be called Windmill Point, held an abundance of wild potatoes and nuts, food that could be quickly harvested and eaten. The Fox hoped that their enemies would think they fled west toward Wisconsin.

The allies did not discover the flight until the following morning, but the rain made it easy to see their direction. A large force of soldiers and Native Americans led by Vincennes caught up with the Fox with Lake St. Clair at their backs. The warriors prepared to make their final stand. Firing from ambush, the Fox killed over 40 of their enemy before Vincennes brought up reinforcements. After four more days of fighting, the Fox warriors offered to surrender if the French would spare their families. Vincennes agreed, providing they lay down their weapons.

Once disarmed, the French and their allies fell upon the Fox with a vengeance. The warriors were literally cut to pieces and their women and children stripped of their clothing. About 100 Fox men were spared so that they could be tortured at leisure. Fortunately for them, on the march back to Fort Ponchartrain, most escaped into the forest. The women and children were not so lucky. They were distributed among the French and their allies as either slaves or captives. The Huron, particularly vindictive and bloodthirsty, amused themselves by torturing or shooting "four or five of them every day" until they had killed off all of their prisoners. French officials at Detroit and Michilimackinac estimated that the Fox and Mascouten lost about 1,000 men, women, and children. With but one brief appearance at Detroit in 1717, the Fox would no longer be a threat to the settlement. However, they did close the fur country west of Lake Michigan to the French from this time on.

PEACE AND WAR

The end of the Fox wars brought a period of relative peace to Michigan until 1744 when conflict in Europe spilled over into the North American continent. Known there as the War of the Austrian Succession and here as King George's War, it would see the English and French pitted against each other, each using their Native American allies to burn, murder, and enslave.

Jacques Charles Sabrevois, Sieur de Bleury, was appointed commandant at Detroit and took up his duties at the end of 1714. Conditions at Fort Ponchartrain did not improve much at this time. The French government did not properly sustain the post and the Company of the Colony, the organization that now controlled the fur trade in Canada, only wanted the country retained because of that trade. In 1716, with a new king on the French throne (Louis XV), the French court cancelled or annulled all of the land grants made by Cadillac, alleging that he had no right or authority to grant them in the first place. Never mind that King Louis XIV did grant him that power. Even though the settlers were left in possession of the land, many people packed up and returned east to Montreal and Quebec. With no clear title to their land, they abandoned their farms and those few that did not leave the area moved into the fort to make their living by trading with the Native Americans and hunting for themselves.

In 1717 Sabrevois was removed from the commandant's post as the term of office usually lasted only three years, and Alphonse de Tonty, Cadillac's old second in command, was appointed in his stead. Tonty, the younger brother of Henry, who was La Salle's right-hand man, was never on a personal sound financial footing. He sold his prospective income from the fur trade to Francois La

Marque and Louis Gastineau. These two, along with three others, tried to prevent other citizens from trading at or anywhere near Detroit. This attempted monopoly made Tonty unpopular and drove morale even further down; even the Native Americans were not happy with the new commandant and joined the French in asking for his recall. The threat of the Huron to leave their village and settle in Ohio, taking the fur trade with them and thereby to the English, had no impact on the government as Tonty served his full term until 1720.

Father Pierre Francois de Charlevoix, a noted French historian and scholar, arrived in Detroit in 1721 to establish a mission among the Huron across the river in Canada. He noted that the place (Detroit) was deserted:

> It is a long time since the importance of this place, still more the beauty of the country about the Straits, has given ground to wish that some considerable settlements were made in this place; this has been tolerably well begun some fifteen years since, but certain causes, of which I am not informed, have reduced it to almost nothing; those who are against it allege, first, that it would bring the trade for the northern furs too near the English, who as they are able to afford their commodities to the Indians cheaper than we, would draw all that trade into the province of New York. Secondly, that the lands near the Straits are not fertile, and that the whole surface to the depth of nine or ten inches consists of sand, below which is hard clay, impenetrable to the water, from whence it happens that the plains and interior parts of the woods are always drowned; that everywhere you see nothing but diminutive, ill grown oaks and hard walnut trees, and that the trees having roots always under water, their fruits ripen very late. These reasons have not been unanswered; it is true that in the neighborhood of Fort Ponchartrain the lands have a mix of sand and that in the forest there are bottoms almost constantly under water, however, these very lands have produced wheat eighteen years successively without the least manure, and you have no great way to go find the finest soil in the world. With respect to woods, without going a great way from the fort, I have seen, as I have been walking, such as may vie with our noblest forest.

Even this tribute from Charlevoix did not attract new

settlers when the government itself was unwilling to encourage them to come. Plans were made to abandon Detroit altogether in the late 1720s, but an unusual foreign demand for beaver fur led the officials in Quebec to change its plans for the settlement. In 1735, 178,000 pounds of beaver was shipped from Quebec, and the increase in trade led them to petition the Crown for more troops to be sent to Detroit at government expense and the commandant be given a yearly salary. Robert Navarre was sent out as intendant of the post and royal notary. He would be the only civil official in Detroit, acting also as justice, surveyor, collector, and sub-delegate to the citizens.

The post began to show new life after the government finally realized that no one would settle there without good title to the land. In 1732 King Louis XV ordered that all Detroit land grants be settled or forfeited. As an inducement to new settlers, families were promised assistance in the form of rations from the military stores, tools, and farm animals. Each head of a family was given farm land. In 1749, 54 heads of families came to Detroit to live. The following year, another 40 arrived and the population of Detroit began to grow.

As Detroit became more populated, the standard of living improved. Crude log houses were replaced with bigger, better-constructed dwellings. Most of the farmers lived on their farms year-round, and a second generation of villages provided more young people within the fort. There was more livestock—pigs and cattle and more horses were available for land transportation. It was at this time that a road was cut through the forest, following the river at least as far as the Rouge River. Also, the fort was expanded, its walls pushed both north and south to accommodate the influx of new settlers. The population, including those in the neighboring farms, totaled around 900 people.

In 1754, the fourth Anglo-French war of the 18th century erupted. Unlike its predecessors, this one began in America and spread to Europe, where it was called the Seven Years War. It was a war over control of territory and began in the Pennsylvania backcountry and had a tremendous effect on the balance of power in Europe. The French and Indian War would end with France losing almost all of its North American empire.

3

A Land Worth Fighting For

On September 8, 1760, the governor-general of New France signed the "Capitulation of Montreal" and formally surrendered the colony, its inhabitants, and all of its territories to Great Britain, effectively ending the French colonial empire in North America.

A few days later, Major Robert Rogers received orders to take possession of Detroit, Michilimackinac, and the entire Northwest and to administer the oath of allegiance to the inhabitants. He left Montreal with 200 soldiers of the 80th Regiment in 15 *bateaux*. At Presque Isle (now Erie, Pennsylvania), he was joined by a detachment of the Royal Americans (60th Reg't.), commanded by Captain Donald Campbell. From there, they journeyed by water to Ashtabula Creek in Ohio, came ashore, and rested. In the first week of November, they were joined by a party of Ottawa who appeared, it seemed, out of nowhere to confront Rogers and his party. Tense at first, the meeting grew more peaceful as gifts were exchanged, and after five days of smoking, drinking, and feasting, the Native Americans learned they were now British subjects. The idea did not sit too well with some of them.

Rogers' fleet arrived at Detroit near the end of the month, having lost only one man to drowning. Rogers sent a runner ahead to alert the French garrison to the news of the surrender. The flotilla landed on the Canadian side of the river not one half mile from the fort. The French commandant, Belestre, received Captain Campbell with all due ceremony and agreed to turn the fort over. On November 29, 1760, the French garrison marched out of Fort Ponchartrain du Detroit with full military honors.

The British Take Control
A new flag meant new changes in the lives of all inhabitants

of Michigan. Detroit went from a French settlement to a British trading post in a conquered territory overnight. Those French who were not amenable to English custom and rules would have to go. Native Americans, who only traded furs with the French, would learn that the English wanted not only their trade goods but the land itself and were willing to drive them off of it.

Captain Donald Campbell assumed command at Detroit after Rogers left two days before Christmas. A wily Scot, Campbell was a veteran of several years of military service before coming to Detroit. In a letter to General Jeffrey Amherst, Campbell described the post:

> The fort is very large and in good repair; there are two bastions toward the water and a large bastion toward the inland. The point of the bastion is a cavalier of wood, on which there are mounted the three-pounders and the small mortars or coehorns. The palisades are in good repair. There is scaffolding around the whole, which is floored only toward the land for want of plank; it is by way of a banquette. There are seventy or eighty houses in the fort, laid out in regular streets. The country is inhabited ten miles on each side of the river and is a most beautiful country. The river here is about nine hundred yards over and very deep. Around the whole village, just within the palisades is a road which is called the "Chemin des Ronde."

When the English took possession of the fort, they found in storage furs worth around $500,000. The intense rivalry between the two countries over the fur trade was ended. The English took steps to increase the trade, and in a few years about 200,000 skins were marketed annually, mostly through Detroit but also through St. Joseph and Michilimackinac. Jeffrey Amherst, who thought the Native Americans crude and uncivilized, stopped giving them presents, food, guns, and ammunition as the French had. This played havoc with the trade and almost destroyed the trust established by the British traders with the Great Lakes tribes.

Disciplined troops now controlled Detroit, and with posted sentinels and day and night perimeter patrols everyday life improved. It wasn't long before Campbell won the confidence of the residents and fraternization

The Northwest Ordinance

Considered to be one of the most significant achievements of the Congress of the Confederation, the Northwest Ordinance of 1787 put the world on notice that the land north of the Ohio River and east of the Mississippi would be settled, but that it would be a part of the United States. Until then, this area had been unavailable for development and settlement. The area opened up by the ordinance was based on boundary lines laid out by Thomas Jefferson in 1784 and provided for the creation of not less than three and not more than five states. In addition, it contained provisions for the advancement of education, the maintenance of civil liberties, and the exclusion of slavery. It certainly accelerated the westward expansion of the country.

became the norm. A cheerful group of 20 men and women gathered at the commandant's house for cards every Saturday night and Campbell wrote to Colonel Henry Bouquet, in command at Fort Pitt, that "the women surpass our expectations, like the rest of America."

As all good things must do, the honeymoon in Detroit ended in the summer of 1762, when Major Henry Gladwin replaced Campbell as commandant. A combat veteran who had been defeated along with General Braddock, Gladwin did not have Campbell's sympathy for the Native Americans or the settlement and was suspicious of French activities in the area. The mindset of the new commander and changes in fur trade policies would soon fan Native American tensions into open, bloody warfare.

PONTIAC'S WAR

British policy prohibited trade anywhere but at British posts. No longer could traders legally conduct business in Native American towns, and it was rather difficult for Native Americans to bring in furs. Presents to them were stopped in peacetime, and as there was no enemy to fight, the prospect of receiving gifts seemed remote. To most Native Americans, this meant British disrespect and the severing of some essential supplies. An influx of settlers,

Field of sunflowers and barn near Wolverine. Randall McCune

especially into the Ohio Valley, dispossessed them of their lands. These factors combined to lead the western tribes to unite and oust the English once and for all from the area.

The great Ottawa chief Pontiac travelled through the region to unite the tribes in this endeavor. From Peche (Peach) Island, just north of Detroit, he called for a grand council of all the tribes to assemble at the Pottawotomie camp on the Ecorse River. On April 27, 1763, he harangued them for hours on the problems with the English. The Pottawomie, Huron, Chippewa, and Ottawa all agreed to the plan and Pontiac's leadership. They would take Detroit

by treachery without endangering their lives. Plans for a general uprising were finalized and runners were sent throughout the territory for the tribes to attack the nearest post and exterminate the English. During the first week in May, posts at Niagara, Sandusky, Presque Isle, Miami, Michilimackinac, St. Joseph, and Pittsburgh would all be targets of attack.

Pontiac met briefly with Major Gladwin on May 1, primarily to get information as to the strength of Detroit's defenses. He told Gladwin that he would return to his camp across the river. There, with almost 60 of his best warriors, they made their final preparations. They were going to carry sawed-off muskets, knives, and toma-hawks beneath their blankets while the rest would take position around the fort.

On the evening preceding the assault, Gladwin was advised of the plan—who told him has remained a matter of debate, as he never divulged his sources. On the morning on May 7, Pontiac and his men, in full regalia, approached the southern land gate and requested a council with the commandant. They were shown into the house of Captain Campbell, where Gladwin and his officers received them, while the rest of the garrison took up positions around the palisades and parade ground. Waiting long enough for his men to get into position, Pontiac stepped outside to give the signal only to find the garrison armed to the teeth and ready to fight. In a rage but under control, he took his leave and stalked out of the fort, followed by his braves.

Once back in camp, Pontiac ordered teams of warriors to kill every English settler or soldier they could lay hands on. By evening, 14 lay dead. Among the slain were George Turnbull, his wife, and two sons; James Fisher, his wife, and one child; two soldiers guarding cattle on Belle Isle; and one Frenchman killed by mistake.

Pontiac moved all his warriors back across the river and laid siege to Detroit. Gladwin responded by closing the water gate and placing water barrels in strategic positions to check the spread of fire. The walls were manned in six-hour shifts by soldiers under his personal direction.

On May 10, the siege began in earnest and was to last until November with much loss of life and property. Requesting a parley and the presence of Captain Campbell, Pontiac laid down his terms, which were severe. The English were to lay down their arms and go to Fort Niagara without their belongings, never to return. He said no more and let everyone leave except Campbell, whom he took prisoner. Seven weeks later, the gray-haired bachelor who so loved the ladies was tomahawked to death, his body tied to a fence and dismembered; then his heart was eaten. A relief expedition from Niagara suffered the same fate, losing 60 of 97 men to Pontiac's warriors.

Native Americans were not very good at siege warfare—it was the white man's way of fighting and not suitable for a warrior. After two months of such tactics, Pontiac had lost a considerable number of men to desertion. The rest were bored, tired, and relaxed. On the morning of July 29 under a thinning fog, a large number of barges carrying 200 reinforcements managed to get to the river gate without being seen. Pontiac had failed to keep Detroit isolated but he was winning throughout the rest of the territory.

MASSACRE AT MICHILIMACKINAC

In late May, a band of Pottawotomie overwhelmed and annihilated the small garrison at Fort St. Joseph. That same week, a band of Chippewa and Sac decided to play a game of "baggatiway," an early form of lacrosse, for a large wager in front of the land gate at Michilimackinac. On June 2, as the game progressed from one goal to the other, the ball was hit over the palisade and into the fort. As the teams rushed through to retrieve it, their women handed them weapons

concealed under their garments. In a flash 16 men, all but one
of them soldiers, were dead and scalped, one of them while
he was still alive. A number of soldiers were taken prisoner,
five later executed. The English traders present that day were
also made prisoner and not harmed. The French inhabitants
there watched the proceedings from the safety of their
homes. The victories were so complete that the British never
permanently re-garrisoned Fort St. Joseph or Sault Ste.
Marie. Michilimackinac was reoccupied in 1764.

THE PROCLAMATION OF 1763

As the siege of Detroit wore on, food supplies for the
Native Americans dwindled and many people left to return
to their hunting grounds to procure food for the winter.
Pontiac was forced to abandon the siege and in early
November was in winter quarters in northern Ohio. The
conflict had left some 2,000 white settlers killed and an
equal number homeless.

As fresh troops reoccupied the abandoned posts, the
government issued the Proclamation of 1763, which set the
boundary beyond which colonists could not settle. The line
ran from the Ottawa River in Canada, along the
Appalachian Mountains, to the southern limit of

Solomon Sibley (1769–1846)

Sibley was born in Sutton, Massachusetts, and studied law,
practicing in Marietta, Ohio, before moving to Detroit in
1796. He was elected to the first legislature of the
Northwest Territory in 1799 and was a delegate to
congress from the territory of Michigan from 1820 to
1823. He was appointed a judge of the supreme court of
Michigan and held that office until compelled to resign in
1836 due to deafness. Sibley was one of only two lawyers
in Detroit in 1797 and was instrumental in passing
legislation incorporating Detroit as a town in 1802 and
served as the town's first mayor under the first city charter.
He was commissioned along with Lewis Cass to negotiate
the Treaty of Chicago with the Ottawa, Potawatomi, and
Chippawa, adding more land to the state.

settlement. Intended to be a temporary measure to help cut military costs and maintain peace with the Native Americans, it closed the entire Ohio River Valley to settlement. This of course alienated the colonists from Pennsylvania and Virginia who had invested in, speculated on, or were actually settling the new land. With too few troops and too large an area to cover, the proclamation was impossible to enforce. It also taught the colonists that they could flaunt royal authority and get away with it, a habit they would put to good use in 1776.

MICHIGAN IN THE REVOLUTION

The problems in the Ohio Valley and elsewhere along the American Atlantic coast had no effect on the French inhabitants of Detroit. On June 22, 1774, the Quebec Act was passed, placing Detroit under the jurisdiction of the Province of Quebec and providing the first civil government for the settlement.

As gunfire erupted across Lexington Green—shots fired by British troops transferred from Michilimackinac—outposts in the West were all placed under what amounted to martial law. Military officers were appointed lieutenant-governors at Michilimackinac, Vincennes, and Detroit. Captain Henry Hamilton arrived to take command at Detroit on November 9, 1775. In his first official report, dated September 2, 1776, Hamilton describes the inhabitants so:

> The enterprising spirit of the trader is likely to crowd out the Canadians and the latter in a few years will be dependant on or bought out by the merchants. The navigation of the lakes in the large vessels is already in the hands of the newcomers. The new settlers manage their farms to the last advantage. The backwardness in the improving of farming has probably been owing to the easy and lazy methods of procuring bare necessities in this settlement, wood was on hand and the inhabitants therefore neglected to raise store and burn lime, which is to be had at their door. The river is plentifully stocked with fish, yet no French family has a seine [net]. Hunting and fowling afford food to numbers who are nearly as lazy as the savage, who are rarely prompted to the chase until hunger pinches them.

The soil is so good that the most ignorant farmer raises good crops. There is no limit to the number of traders permitted here and the unworthy and dishonest ones impose on the savages and cheat them.

With this attitude, both the French and Native American inhabitants were in for a trying time. Hamilton spent most of 1775 and 1776 improving the defenses of Detroit against real and imagined enemies. He abused his judicial powers and several cases of petty theft ended in execution. In June Hamilton received orders from London to begin a widespread Native American war against rebellious colonists living in the Ohio Valley. For the next several years the valley would see the torch and scalping knife.

To help stop these depredations, congress ordered George Rogers Clark to outfit a force at Fort Pitt to capture or destroy Vincennes and Detroit. Believing Detroit too strong to take, Clark marched into Native American country and captured Kaskaskia and Vincennes in the early part of July. Hamilton decided to recapture both posts to restore British prestige. He retook Vincennes (which was held by two men), but politely surrendered when faced by Clark's army and spent the rest of the war as a prisoner in Virginia.

The English reaction to these circumstances resulted in the construction of Fort Lernoult at Detroit and the dismantling of Fort Michilimackinac. The new fort at Detroit was on a small hill just north of the French post and the two were connected by a palisade wall. Michilimackinac was moved to Mackinac Island and reassembled. Detroit continued to be staging area for Native American raids into Kentucky and Virginia, while Mackinac served as a collection point for furs and supplies to and from the West for the remainder of the American Revolution. The Treaty of Paris, signed in 1783, awarded the territory to the new United States, but the English refused to leave until forced to by the arrival of an American army in 1796. Michigan had finally become a United States territory.

AMERICAN TAKEOVER

On July 11, 1796, two small schooners carrying Captain Moses Porter and 65 men of the 1st US Infantry Regiment, tacked in and tied up at the King's Wharf. At noon the Union Jack was hauled down and the Stars and Stripes was raised over Fort Lernoult. Michigan had its third owner in over 90 years. Two days later Colonel John Francis Hamtramck marched in with the rest of the Regiment, almost 400 soldiers.

In mid-August, no less a personage than General Anthony Wayne arrived in Detroit to establish army headquarters. He brought along with him territorial secretary Winthrop Sargent, who established the civil government. On August 15, 1796, Wayne County was organized; named in honor of the general, the county consisted of nearly all of Michigan and parts of Ohio, Indiana, and Wisconsin. In December it was divided up into townships and officials were appointed for each: St. Clair, Hamtramck, Detroit, and Sargent. Along with Sault Ste. Marie and Mackinac, other settlements included Frenchtown (soon to be renamed Monroe), the Moravian settlement along the Clinton River near present-day Mount Clemens, and a small group at Port Huron. Detroit, the largest at this time, consisted of the fort and citadel, a wharf, about 100 houses, shops, taverns, and St. Anne's Church crowded behind the fort's walls. Ribbon farms extended both north and south of the fort as far as the St. Clair River and the Rouge River. An estimated 500 people lived in the fort, with another 2,100 on the nearby farms.

Monroe piers, 1915
Monroe County Historical Commission

THE TERRITORY OF MICHIGAN

Though the American government was unable to occupy its newly acquired territory until 1796, it had made provision for governing it. The first American election was held in December of 1798, and Solomon Sibley was elected to the Northwest Territory's legislative council. His opponent was pro-British and Sibley gave voters free liquor on election day—either fact would solidify victory. He was joined a year later by two other representatives, Jacob Visger and Francois Joncare de Chabert. The legislative council met in Cincinnati, Ohio, over 300 miles away.

The citizens that they represented were quite a diverse group. Josep Moore, a Quaker from Philadelphia, remarked in 1793, "The inhabitants of the town are as great a mixture, I think, as ever I knew in any one place. English, Scotch, Irish, Dutch (German), French, Americans from different states, with Black and Yellow, and seldom clear of Indians of different tribes in the daytime."

The town of Detroit continued to be a center of commercial activity, primarily due to the still prospering fur trade. It was well supplied with taverns and stores where travelers could lodge, quench their thirst, and trade their goods. The majority of these new entrepreneurs were not French but others who had married into the old French families. The spiritual needs of the town were amply seen to by Father Gabriel Richard and the Reverend David Bacon, who ministered to the Catholics and Protestants, respectively. Both men were very active in the community, and Bacon and his wife opened separate schools for boys and girls in 1801.

The following year, Detroit was incorporated as a town. The charter, enacted on January 18 by the Northwest Territory General Assembly, provided for a governing board of five trustees and a secretary, assessor, tax collector, and marshal. The board adopted a fire code as well as ordinances prohibiting horse racing on city streets and regulating the price and weight of bread, which was baked in public ovens, and levied the very first city tax, assessing 25 cents upon each person over 21 years of age.

On January 11, 1805, President Thomas Jefferson approved a congressional act forming Michigan Territory and appointed William Hull the territorial governor. A

Massachusetts native, Hull was a Yale graduate, lawyer, and a courageous veteran of the Revolution. In his mid-50s, Hull had considerable ability but absolutely no knowledge of frontier life and its particular problems.

Along with Hull, Jefferson appointed Augustus Woodward, Frederick Bates, and John Griffin as judges and Stanley Griswold as territorial secretary. All of these men were Easterners, with the exception of Bates who served in the army at Detroit in 1800. Michigan was to governed by a curious arrangement of a governor and judges committee.

On June 11, 1805, a few days before the arrival of these men, a fire broke out in John Harvey's stable next to his bakery. In a little less than two hours, the entire town was being consumed by flames. Amazingly, no one was hurt but nothing was left except some stone structures and chimneys.

As residents were accommodated in tents on the commons or on farms along the river, discussion commenced on how to rebuild. Judge Woodward persuaded Hull to postpone the rebuilding until a comprehensive plan could be drawn up. With Congressional approval, he implemented the Woodward Plan and Detroit became the territorial capital in 1806.

NATIVE AMERICAN LAND CESSIONS

The first order of business in any new government was to obtain new land for settlement, so Hull called for a council with the Native Americans. On November 17, 1807, the Treaty of Detroit was signed, ceding to the United States most of southeastern Michigan. The Native Americans in Michigan reluctantly went about their business, hoping to not have to bother with the whites again.

In 1808 Hull was reappointed to his third term as territorial governor and suffered through a war scare with Great Britain and a congress reluctant to appropriate any funds for the defense of Michigan. The governor repeatedly petitioned Washington for more troops and a Great Lakes naval presence. The lack of support would prove disastrous. In the spring of 1808, Father Gabriel Richard presented his plan for a primary school system to educate both white and Native American children. Hull encouraged him to go to Washington and present the plan to Jefferson. The

The Woodward Plan

When fire raced through and destroyed the town of Detroit in 1805, only one building was left standing. The territorial supreme court judge, Augustus Woodward, presented a plan similar to the layout of Washington, DC, for the rebuilding of Detroit. It called for wide streets, squares, and circuses or open spaces of ground, and wide lots of 5,000 square feet with an alley or lane coming off the rear of each lot. It was an expandable plan and the first unit can still be seen today. The base of this unit parallels the river for 4,000 feet, with its apex at Grand Circus Park. The intersection of avenues is seen at Campus Martius.

president told Congress to provide support for the Native American venture, but that order fell on deaf ears. Richard returned to Detroit but not before purchasing a piano, an organ, and a printing press, along with equipment and a printer named James Miller. On August 31, 1809, the first and probably only issue of Michigan's first newspaper, *The Michigan Essay Or Impartial Observer*, was printed. It was a four-page paper, printed in both French and English, and no one knows why it was discontinued. Only five known copies are extant.

THE WAR OF 1812

In January of 1812, Detroit felt the tremors of an earthquake, which should have served as an omen of the tremors of war soon to effect all of Michigan. Relations with Britain had deteriorated to such a low point that Hull was summoned to Washington while on leave in the East to discuss the protection of the frontier. He was asked to take command of the Army of the Northwest, an army that did not as yet exist. At first he refused, claiming ill health (he had suffered a stroke recently) and again because he believed that Detroit could not be held unless the United States controlled Lake Erie. He finally accepted after being allowed to keep his post as governor and draw both salaries.

Gabriel Richard

Priest, pioneer, patriot, civic leader, publisher, teacher, congressman, patron of the arts; Father Gabriel Richard could claim all of these titles. He escaped the French Revolution in 1791 and served in the Illinois mission for six years before coming to Detroit in 1798. He ministered to Protestants as well as Catholics before there was a Protestant ministry in Detroit, placing him well ahead of his time. He brought the first printing press to the city and, in addition to the first newspaper in Michigan, he printed many books, the first being *The Child's Spelling Book*.

Appointed and confirmed a brigadier general by Congress, Hull was to collect his army and invade Canada from Detroit as one part of a three-pronged assault. He was also to safeguard Michigan, counteract British influence with the Native Americans, and gain control of Lake Erie without ships. It was a plan destined to fail.

The Army of the Northwest would eventually total 2,075 men, mostly untrained, undisciplined Ohio militia, and the 4th US Infantry. His Ohio subordinate commanders, Duncan McArthur and Lewis Cass, would quibble over who outranked whom and continually undermine Hull's command. In August, after invading Canada then withdrawing with no support and under the threat of a massive Native American uprising, Hull surrendered Detroit to the British.

The loss of Detroit shocked the people of the Northwest Territory and the administration in Washington. Finding a convenient scapegoat in Hull, a board of inquiry found him guilty of cowardice and neglect of duty. Sentenced to be executed in 1814, Hull was pardoned by President James Monroe because of Hull's age and previous war service record. To this day, his reputation is reviled.

Additional efforts to retake Michigan in early 1813 failed and it wasn't until the United States gained control on Lake Erie that the state would return to US control. Oliver Hazard Perry's decisive victory at Put-in-Bay

Steam threshing, Erie, MI, date unknown
Monroe County Historical Commission

allowed the land forces under General William Henry Harrison to march in and defeat the British at the Battle of the Thames in Canada.

The Treaty of Ghent, Belgium, ended the War of 1812 and restored all conquered territory to both belligerents. The war left Michigan devastated. In Detroit a shortage of food and an outbreak of cholera took its toll on the inhabitants. Crops had been destroyed and livestock killed or driven off. Most of the surplus wood was gone as fence rails, barns, and sheds were torn down and burned for warmth by both armies. But Michigan's place as an American territory was secured and the rebuilding process would begin.

4

BUILDING A STATE

Lewis Cass returned to Michigan in 1814 as military governor, appointed by General William Henry Harrison. He wasted no time in securing his appointment as civilian governor and superintendent over some 30,000 Native Americans residing in the territory. In the fall of that year, fellow lawyer William Woodbridge of Ohio was appointed secretary. He wrote to General Duncan McArthur at Detroit asking for information about conditions in the area before accepting the appointment. McArthur wrote back suggesting he visit the town and judge for himself but couldn't resist voicing his opinion.

According to General McArthur:

> …it would be to the advantage of Government to remove every inhabitant of the Territory, pay for the improvements and reduce them to ashes, leaving nothing but the Garrison posts. From my observation, the Territory appears to be not worth defending and merely a den for Indians and traitors. The banks of the Detroit River are handsome, but nine-tenths of the land in the Territory is unfit for cultivation.

In spite of McArthur's words, Woodbridge accepted the position and moved to Detroit. In April, 1815, he wrote to Secretary of State James Monroe, explaining the condition of the people, stating, "the pressure of the war has indeed been severe upon them…. [N]o equal position of the community, I am confident, have been so greatly harassed or so greatly distressed." He also stated that the inhabitants had been systematically plundered by the Native Americans throughout the course of the war.

Michigan was indeed in a desolated condition and it was the responsibility of the new officials to improve it.

Cass and Woodbridge were New Englanders, but both had lived long enough in the West to understand the people and their needs. Both of them were relatively young, being in their thirties. What was needed was land, transportation, and settlers.

MORE LAND FOR SETTLEMENT

Governor Cass was eager to promote the prosperity of the territory. In order to do that, he had to have land to offer to new settlers. As Indian superintendent, he had the authority to sign treaties and acquire land. The first order of business was to make peace with the tribes. This was accomplished on September 8, 1815, when the hatchet was buried in a colorful ceremony and the Treaty of Spring Wells was signed. No land cessions were involved, but a formal peace was made with all of the Native Americans in Michigan, Indiana, and Ohio. Two years later, Cass and McArthur signed the Treaty of Fort Meigs, which involved cessions mostly in Ohio but included an area in Michigan, now Hillsdale County.

THE TREATY OF SAGINAW

In January of 1819, Cass notified the secretary of war that he believed the time was right for obtaining a land cession in the Saginaw Valley and that the Native Americans in the region must either be relocated west or be placed on reservations surrounded by white settlements. By the early spring, he was authorized to make a treaty.

There was a trading post in operation at Saginaw run by Louis Campau. At the governor's request, Cass erected some small buildings for the official party and cleared an area for the treaty council. Cass and his party traveled overland from Detroit, while the supplies and one company of the 3rd US Infantry traveled by boat. More than 1,000 Native Americans, mostly Chippewa, were present. Over the course of the next 10 days, three formal councils were held to hammer out the agreement. On September 24, 1819, the treaty was signed, ceding to the United States over 6 million acres of land from the western border of the 1801 Treaty of Detroit north to Thunder Bay River, then south on a diagonal line to the present city of Kalamazoo. It was the largest land grant in Michigan up to that time.

Land Development

Starting in the fall of 1815, Cass began to lay out the county system in Michigan, redrawing Wayne county's boundaries to near their present-day ones. In 1817 in honor of President James Monroe's visit to Detroit, the city and county of Monroe were created. One year later, Michilimackinac, Brown, and Crawford counties were delineated, the latter two being west of Lake Michigan, in present-day Wisconsin. Still, no settlers came in sufficient numbers.

After the War of 1812, the United States government decided to reward its soldiers with land warrants. Two million acres of Michigan land were to be set aside and surveyed for this purpose. The surveying began in the summer of 1815, which unfortunately was an unusually wet one. As part of the bounty lands were in the watershed of many rivers, surveyors repeatedly sent back bad reports on the useless, marshy lands. An official report went out stating that not one acre in a 100 could be cultivated and suggested that the bounty lands in Michigan be transferred to Illinois and Missouri. People stayed away from the state in droves.

Governor Cass attacked the report as inaccurate and demanded that a resurvey be done. It soon became evident that the original report was wrong. In 1818 the Federal Government opened a land office in Detroit for the sale of tracts that had been surveyed. The misunderstanding actually helped, as the land speculators stayed away and more permanent settlers purchased land.

As some settlers began arriving in Michigan, new towns were founded, usually along the old Native American trails leading from Detroit. Founders of a town chose a spot along a river or creek where a dam could be constructed to provide power for saw or grist mills.

John Hunter made the first land entry at Birmingham, in Oakland County. Mount Clemens, surveyed in 1795, was first platted in 1818 and became the county seat that same year. Settlers from western New York purchased land at Rochester. A group of men from Detroit laid out the town of Pontiac, on the Saginaw Trail.

Major John Biddle acquired 2,200 acres after a survey and auction around the present-day city of Wyandotte while settlers were beginning to cultivate land around Dearborn. Again in Oakland County, Governor Cass

South Haven South Pier light, located on Lake Michigan
David Vaughn

camped under a huge oak tree while out on an inspection
tour, a tree which reminded him of the story of the Royal
Oak in Scotland—so he named the place. Ever so slowly,
Michigan grew.

Governor Cass Explores the Territory

On January 24, 1820, the US Senate confirmed Lewis Cass
for another three-year term as governor of Michigan
Territory. That same month, they approved his planned
expedition to explore and map the territory along with a
military escort and $1000 to help defray expenses.
Topographical engineer David P. Douglas and mineralogist
Henry Rowe Schoolcraft were ordered to report to Detroit.
Cass carefully assembled his crew as he truly wanted this to
be a scientific expedition. In all, the Cass party totaled 40
men. They would travel in three birch bark canoes, 35 feet
in length and six feet wide in the middle. Ordered from the
Native Americans at Saginaw Bay, they could carry four
tons of cargo yet be easily carried across portages by four
men. Cass had his decorated with a bright red awning.

The expedition set out from Detroit late in the
afternoon of May 24, 1820, and arrived at Michilimackinac
on June 6. While the canoes were refitted, Schoolcraft
studied the mineral deposits on nearby St. Martin's Island.
Their next stop was Sault Ste. Marie and a meeting with the
Chippewa, who were unwilling to cede any land for a fort.
After Cass stood down the younger, defiant braves, the plot
of land was given and in 1822 Fort Brady was constructed.

The governor's expedition continued into Lake
Superior along the south shore where each day revealed
new wonders to the party: the extensive marshland of the
Grand Marais; the sand dunes at Grand Sable; and the
Pictured Rocks, which impressed Schoolcraft enough to
write that they provided "some of the most sublime and
commanding views in nature."

Ten days after leaving the Sault, the expedition
completed the portage across the Keweenaw Peninsula,
passing through the Portage River and Portage Lake. The
tour continued to the western extremity of Lake Superior,
past the Porcupine Mountains and through the Apostle
Islands. The next goal was to discover the source of the
Mississippi River. They reached the Falls of St. Anthony

(the site of present-day Minneapolis) on July 30, where they received a warm welcome from Colonel Henry Leavenworth, commander at the post. Finally arriving at Green Bay, the party split up, some of the men examining the shore of Lake Michigan north to the Straits of Mackinac and Cass and the others proceeding south to Fort Dearborn (present-day Chicago).

Cass left the party there to complete the survey of the southern end of the Lake and proceeded on horseback to return to Detroit over the Sauk Trail (now US12). He was back at his starting point on September 13, having traveled a total of 4,200 miles. Ten days later, Schoolcraft and the others returned. Cass' dealings with the Native Americans were successful, with the exception of his newly acquired nickname of "Os-Kotchee" or "Big Belly." The government published a report of the expedition which brought much needed attention to Michigan.

IMPROVEMENTS AND GROWTH

In order to divert the stream of immigrants bypassing the territory and settling elsewhere, improvements would have to be made. One important area was transportation—how one got to and around Michigan. On August 27, 1818, the arrival of the steamboat *Walk-in-the-Water* on her inaugural run from Buffalo, New York, signaled the beginning of a faster trip to Michigan from points east. Others would soon follow. The completion of the Erie Canal in 1825 turned a trip of weeks into one of days from Albany on the Hudson River to points west.

Governor Cass induced the US Congress to appropriate funds to build roads in Michigan and several were begun in the 1820s. All of them followed old Native American trails, which had been in use for centuries. The first one connected Detroit with Fort Meigs at Perrysburg, Ohio (now US25). Post roads were built from Detroit to Pontiac and Mt. Clemens. In 1822 public stagecoaches began service from Detroit. Roads would determine the direction of Michigan's settlement as first way stations then small towns were established along the route. Two years later, with an additional appropriation from Congress, the survey of the Great Sauk Trail was begun for a road from Detroit to Chicago. That road (I-94) would be completed in

Lewis Cass (1782-1866)

Lewis Cass was born in Exeter, New Hampshire, and attended Exeter academy before moving to Delaware with his parents in 1799 where he taught school. He moved to the Northwest territory in 1801 and settled near Zanesville, Ohio, where he studied law, served in the state legislature, and was marshal for the district of Ohio from 1807 to 1812, when he resigned to enlist in the army. Emerging from the War of 1812 as a brigadier general, Cass served as military and civil governor from 1813 to 1831 when President Andrew Jackson appointed him secretary of war and served until 1836. Cass was elected to the US Senate in 1845 and served until 1848 when he resigned, having been nominated for president of the United States. Unsuccessful in his bid for the presidency, he was reelected to the senate in 1849 to fill the vacancy caused by his own resignation and served until 1857, when President James Buchanan appointed him secretary of state. He served until his retirement in 1860, returning to Detroit and engaging in literary pursuits until his death in 1866. Cass is buried in Detroit's Elmwood Cemetery.

1835 and two stagecoaches per week would make the round trip. The Fort Gratiot Road from Detroit to Port Huron was built during this time period, along with the Territorial Road, branching off the Chicago Road at Dearborn (US12). The last road to be constructed during the Territorial period was surveyed from Detroit to Grand Rapids in 1832. Five years later it was finished as far as Howell (US16). All of these roads led from or to Detroit.

GROWING METROPOLIS

The City of Detroit had been growing steadily since the territory was reacquired by the United States. In 1817 the city's first regularly published newspaper, *The Detroit Gazette*, was founded. It was printed in French and English and had fewer than 100 subscribers. That same year, the City Library, the Bank of Michigan, the Detroit Musical Society, and the first charitable society, the Moral and

Currency from "The Bank of Battle Creek," established 1836
Willard Library (Battle Creek, MI)

Humane Society, whose aim was to suppress vice and report on children in need of education, came into being.

The first Protestant church building in Michigan was dedicated in 1818 near the Rouge River, and the cornerstone for a new St. Anne's Church at Larned and Bates Streets was laid. Two years later in 1820, the first Protestant church building in Detroit was dedicated on Woodward Avenue, just north of Larned. The Reverend John Monteith was pastor. That year, Detroit's population was just under 1,500 and Michigan's just under 9,000 souls.

At Griswold and Jefferson Avenues in Detroit, the territorial capitol and courthouse were constructed; in 1823 Congress granted Michigan a legislative council, transferring government from the governor and judges to the governor and legislators. The people were to elect 18 candidates, from whom the president would select nine. Most Detroiters greeted the change with delight and readied to elect a new congressional delegate and a council. The delegate election proved to be a bitter one, with no clearly established political party lines. The principle candidates were Austin Wing, John Biddle, and John R. Williams. Then at the prodding of some of his parishioners, Father Richard decided to throw his hat into the ring. He was well-known in Michigan and would certainly have the French Catholic vote, which Williams, a Catholic himself, had hoped to gain. For the first time, the election would be open to all counties of Michigan.

The official count held at the council house on October 23 revealed that Richard had 444 votes to Biddle's 335; the rest were divided among the four other candidates. Biddle

Fort Brady

On July 6, 1822, a battalion of American troops under Colonel Hugh Brady reached the Sault, thereby reasserting American control over this region as a result of the Treaty of the Sault made by Lewis Cass in 1820. Fort Brady was built by the end of that year and remained until it was moved to a new site in 1893 by the order of General Phil Sheridan. It is located on Water Street in Sault Ste. Marie, Chippewa County. Fort Brady was originally built on the grounds of an old French fort (Ft. Repentigny).

contested the election on the grounds that Richard's naturalization was invalid and that he had not been a citizen for four years. The House Committee on Elections ruled in Richard's favor and he become the first and only priest in the history of Congress.

Almost 25,000 votes were cast for council members, the average voter casting 15 of his authorized 18 votes. Receiving votes were 123 men, but only 18 received more than 500 each. The highest nine were one from each county except Crawford and there were two from Monroe and Oakland counties. Cass suggested that the highest nine be appointed, as the majority of counties were represented. Congress confirmed the first nine on February 4, 1824, and reappointed Cass to his fifth three-year term as governor.

On June 7, 1824, the first legislative council of Michigan convened in Detroit. That August, a city charter was adopted, providing for local government by a mayor and a common council consisting of five men, all elected by the people. The charter also created the offices of recorder and city clerk appointed by the council. On September 6, 1824, the people of Detroit elected John R. Williams as their first mayor.

TOWN DEVELOPMENT

The latter half of the 1820s saw a growing number of towns, coinciding with the improvement of roads in the territory. At the confluence of the Huron River and the Chicago Road, Ypsilanti was founded in 1824. Saline,

Pictured Rocks

Mineral-stained sandstone cliffs rise dramatically from Lake Superior at the Pictured Rocks National Lakeshore. The 70,000-acre park follows the south shore of Lake Superior for 42 miles. The cliffs are shaped by wind, ice, and the pounding waves and colored in shades of brown, tan, and green by the iron, manganese, limonite, and copper in the water. The sculptured rocks have various names, such as Miner's Castle, Battleship Row, Indian Head, Lover's Leap, and the Colored Caves, among others.

Jonesville, Coldwater, Sturgis, Clinton, and Niles were all set up along the Chicago Road by 1830. In 1832 the road was at least passable as far as Niles, and just three years later stagecoaches were making the run from Detroit to Chicago.

Tecumseh and Adrian, both in Lenawee County, were founded and prospered. At the former, a sawmill, tannery gristmill, and a furniture factory were soon running. Adrian had a sawmill and gristmill, both powered by the two branches of the River Raisin.

As plans for the Territorial Road were finalized, towns appeared along the route. The first was Ann Arbor, co-founded in 1824 by two men whose wives' names were Ann. Jackson was next in 1829 and named for the serving president. 1831 saw the first settler of Albion, then Marshall, where Rice Creek joins the Kalamazoo River, and Battle Creek, where two Native Americans fought it out with two members of the surveying party. Titus Bronson of Connecticut built his log cabin on Kalamazoo River in 1829 and platted the village of Bronson two years later. The village was renamed Kalamazoo, after the Native American word for "reflecting river." The proposed terminus for the Territorial Road was at St. Joseph, first occupied by La Salle in 1679 and finally platted as a village in 1831.

Villages also sprang up along the route of the Grand River Road. Quakers from Farmington, New York, founded Quakertown in Oakland County in 1824; they were given a post office named Farmington two years later.

In Livingston County, Ore Creek was founded in 1832; in 1838, it was renamed Brighton by popular approval. Howell was next, though it was first called Livingston Center from its location in the county.

A fur trader named McKenzie located his camp at the Rapids of the Grand River in 1820, but it wasn't until Louis Campau bought the city's present-day business district for a whopping $90 in 1831 that development began. With abundant water power available and access to Lake Michigan, Grand Rapids had potential.

Grand Haven, at the mouth of the Grand River, started as the headquarters of the American Fur Company in the early 1820s. There was a store, a warehouse, and not much else until 1834, when the village was platted and named for its location.

With the towns came stores, mills, schools, churches, and newspapers—all of the elements of civilization. The Territorial Council in 1827 passed a law that required every township with a population of 50 or more to hire a schoolteacher. Various courses were also offered by many churches in Sunday schools. By 1837 at least 10 towns in the state had one or more thriving newspapers.

STORMY ROAD TO STATEHOOD

The 5th US census, taken in 1830, revealed a total of 31,639 non-Native American people living in Michigan Territory,

The Old Sauk Trail

The Old Sauk Trail originally ran easterly across Illinois from Rock Island to the Illinois River at about where Peru is now, paralleled the north bank of that river to Joliet and then easterly to Valparaiso, Indiana. From there it angled northeasterly to LaPorte and on across southern Michigan passing through Niles, Three Rivers, Jonesville, Clinton, and Ypsilanti to Detroit. For centuries, the Native Americans traveled it in single file on missions of peace and war until they had beaten a pathway deep into the soil. They were partial to low ridges but went around hills, lakes, swamps, and places too thick with underbrush and that is why the Sauk Trail is so crooked.

including 32 slaves, 10 of whom were females. All but three of these slaves lived in the area west of the peninsula. There were 261 free African-Americans, mostly in Wayne County. The free white population consisted of 18,168 males and 13,178 females. About half of each were between the ages of 20 and 50; there were 3,124 females between 10 and 20 years of age. Only four counties had more than 3,000 people: Wayne, 6,781; Oakland, 4,911; Washtenaw, 4,542; and Monroe, 3,187. Michigan officials were disappointed in the totals. They were expecting the Lower Peninsula to exceed 30,000 people and were about 500 short of that goal, too short to qualify for statehood.

The decade was filled with developments and improvements in the territory. The Great Western Stage Company began service from Detroit to Tecumseh twice a week and soon after extended service to Chicago via Niles. Also, Detroit received regular mail service from Ohio three times per week.

Not yet a state, Michigan already had a core group of citizens interested in reform. The last execution in Michigan took place in Detroit on September 24, 1830, when Stephen G. Simmons, a tavern keeper in Wayne, was hanged for killing his wife in a drunken rage. Elizabeth M. Chandler founded the Logan Female Anti-Slavery Society in Lenawee County. This was the first formal organization of its kind in Michigan, although Mrs. Laura Haviland began her activities at around the same time. A Baptist minister, Reverend Abel Bingham, organized the St. Mary's Temperance Society at the Sault. A similar society began in Detroit. The Detroit Female Seminary was established in 1830 and opened in 1836, with William Kirkland as principal. This was one of the first schools for girls but unfortunately closed in 1842. Michigan's permanent school system was yet to be.

After 18 years as governor of Michigan Territory, Lewis Cass resigned in order to become President Jackson's secretary of war. Also heading to Washington, DC, was Territorial Secretary John T. Mason and his son, Stevens. The elder Mason resigned, stating the need to go to Texas to look after some land claims there. He asked Jackson to appoint his son in his stead, as he had been assisting him and knew the duties well. Jackson did just that and upon Cass' resignation, Stevens

View of Langley covered bridge near Centreville
Travel Michigan

Caroline Kirkland (1801–1864)

An educated eastern woman, Caroline Kirkland was a contemporary of Edgar Allan Poe who followed her husband west when he had become "land hungry" and invested heavily in a new settlement to be built out of the marshes near Detroit. She published her autobiographical novel of their misadventures in New York in 1839 under the pseudonym "Mrs. Mary Clavers, an actual settler." The book, entitled *A New Home, Who'll Follow?*, unfortunately made its way back to town and angered her neighbors.

Thomson Mason became acting governor at the ripe old age of 19, not quite old enough to vote.

News of these events reached Detroit before Mason did. The people held a public meeting, duly formed a committee to investigate the situation, and sent a memorial to the president. Signed by 160 citizens, it objected to the fact that Mason was too young to vote and own property. Mason wisely responded in the public press, saying that he had been helping his father for quite some time and knew the duties and that a governor would be appointed soon, making his duties routine. In a separate report he sent to the secretary of state, Mason said that only thirteen of the signers were Jackson supporters; 46 supported Henry Clay and 22 were complete strangers.

As the parties dickered, Jackson appointed George B. Porter of Pennsylvania as governor on August 6, 1831. Not arriving until September, Porter returned to Pennsylvania within three weeks on business and the whole controversy began again. Porter took ill back in his home state and was still not recovered upon his return to Michigan. Mason, acting as governor, had to convene the legislative council, enticing an opposition newspaper, *The Emigrant*, of Ann Arbor to call him "an illiterate, vulgar youth."

Mason handled the council well, got an important piece of legislation passed, and saw his popularity grow. Unfortunately, a cholera epidemic struck Detroit, brought there by a ship carrying US troops to fight in the Black Hawk War on July 4, 1832. By July 18, 58 cases of cholera were reported, resulting in 28 deaths. The disease spread to the interior but was, for the most part, contained, though not before claiming the life of Gabriel Richard as one of its last victims. The town of Marshall suffered the most; out of 70 residents, 18 were taken ill and eight died.

Once these threats subsided, the citizens of Michigan once again turned their attention to the statehood issue. This time there were distinct party lines. The Whigs and Conservative Democrats were opposed by the Liberal Democrats. The Liberals, led by Mason, were in favor of statehood and reform. Their support came from the poorer classes, new immigrants from western New York, and the few foreigners who began to settle in Michigan. The conservatives opposed statehood. Led by local office holders, the wealthy, and the educated, they felt that the first step toward statehood should be taken by Congress, who paid the bills while Michigan was a territory. Many of them refused to vote in the upcoming election, which was to decide whether or not to form a state government.

The election held on October 2, 1832, found 1,817 in favor and 1,190 opposed to forming a government. In January of 1833, a petition was duly drawn up and sent to congress requesting authorization to form a constitution and a

Stevens Thomson Mason
(1811-1843)

Stevens Thomson Mason was born in Virginia in 1811 to a rich and powerful family whose paternal grandfather was a US senator and whose family could count James Monroe as a friend and neighbor. Stevens' father, John T. Mason, had an overwhelming desire to head west, and the family moved to Lexington, Kentucky, in 1812, where he was at first quite successful. However, John was inept at business and soon lost everything until he secured an appointment as secretary of Michigan territory in 1830. The move to Detroit came as a shock to the genteel Virginians, and it was the son who protected the father from the backroom political schemes until John tired of the intrigue and secured a mission to Mexico, leaving Stevens to become secretary and then governor.

The State Seal

The Great Seal of the state of Michigan was inspired by the seal used by the Hudson Bay Company. Michigan's second governor, Lewis Cass, presented the idea to the constitutional convention and it was accepted on June 2, 1835. At the center of the seal, there is an image of a man standing at the tip of the peninsula, rifle at the ready, watching the sun rise. A moose and an elk stand keeping the shield in place and an eagle adds to the majesty. The motto, "Tuebor," means "I will defend."

government. After over a year had passed, Congress acted on the petition, rejecting it and extending the territorial boundary to the Missouri River. Several problems still had to worked out: the boundary of the state, the creation of a new territory for the western area, and whether or not to include Michilimackinac and the Sault in the new state. Congress did authorize the demolition of the stockade walls in Detroit and built a new arsenal to store and repair weapons at the confluence of the Rouge River and the Chicago Road. It consisted of 10 buildings, some of them brick, and was named the Dearborn arsenal—a town soon grew up around it.

On Sunday, July 6, 1834, Governor John Porter, age 43, died after a four-day illness and Mason was once again acting governor, this time without much opposition. In November, he announced to the council that over 85,000 people lived in the Peninsula of Michigan, thus qualifying it for statehood. Mason urged the council to provide for electing delegates to a constitutional convention. The council obliged and the convention convened on May 11, 1835, in Detroit with 89 delegates from around the territory. By June 24, the constitution was written, consisting of a brief preamble, thirteen articles, and a schedule of procedure toward a state government. Propositions to change the state name to Huron, abolish imprisonment for debt, and enforce a minimum age of 35 years for governor had all failed to pass. On October 5, voters approved the constitution and elected state and national officials.

The first session of the state legislature took place in Detroit on November 2. The following day, Stevens T. Mason was inaugurated as the state's first governor, despite congressional refusal to grant statehood. The boundary dispute appeared to be the major problem.

The exact location of the southern boundary of Michigan had been in dispute for some time. The boundary line was to run from the southern end of Lake Michigan across to Maumee Bay, except that when the line was drawn, cartographers had the end of Lake Michigan too far north. The dispute with Ohio grew so hot that the militia was called out. Luckily, the only casualty of the Toledo War was a pig.

Finally, on April 2, 1836, the US Congress passed an act admitting Michigan to the Union providing that the Ohio boundary was accepted. At first, the legislature rejected the terms. In December the Convention of Assent (also called the "frost-bitten convention") held in Ann Arbor accepted the terms for admission. In exchange for giving up the Toledo Strip, Michigan gained the entire Upper Peninsula.

On January 26, 1837, Michigan was finally admitted as the 26th State, with the capitol at Detroit. After nearly three years of political bickering, debate, and armed confrontation, a new star was added to the Stars and Stripes.

The Toledo War

Led by 22-year-old Governor Stevens T. Mason, a small 250-man group of volunteers marched toward Toledo to defend their territory from an Ohio takeover. Refusing to negotiate was Ohio Governor Robert Lucas who successfully lobbied in Washington to gain the strip of land which he organized into a county and named after himself. The war was on. The Ohio legislature voted a military budget of $300,000, which Michigan countered with a budget of $315,000. Mason and his "troops" arrested some Ohio officials, captured nine surveyors, and mistakenly shot to death one pig. President Jackson stepped in and the war ended. Congress held Michigan statehood hostage until it agreed to Ohio's claims and ended up with the valuable lands of the Upper Peninsula."

5

Exploiting Natural Resources: Copper, Iron, and Lumber

Wildcats, Railroads, and Patriots

The brand new 26th state contained about 175,000 people, many of them descendants of French-Canadians pioneers. But the majority of the inhabitants had come from New England and New York, with a few immigrants from Germany and Ireland. Twenty-two counties were organized, all but two, Mackinac and Chippewa, in the Lower Peninsula. By 1840 four tiers of the southernmost counties were complete and Saginaw County was the first filled in the fifth tier.

By 1842 all of Michigan's land belonged to the US government, the last Native American treaties being settled, and plenty of land was available. Land offices around the state were doing a booming business. For example, in 1836 the Kalamazoo office transferred 1,634,511 acres into private hands at a cost of $2,043,866. Everybody was going land crazy. More than four million acres were sold from offices in Detroit, Monroe, Flint, and Ionia—greater than in any other state. Money was plentiful, especially paper money.

At the same time, Michigan embarked on a massive internal improvement project. Plans were made for three railroads and two canals to span the state from east to west. But too much enthusiasm and too much political pressure led to too many projects.

The Erie & Kalamazoo Railroad received its charter in 1833, making it the first in the state. It began to operate a single horse-drawn coach on tracks from Toledo to Adrian in 1836. The new roads were to go from Monroe to New Buffalo on Lake Michigan; another from Detroit to St. Joseph; and the third from Port Huron to Grand Rapids. In

75

Hugh Brady (1768–1851)

Hugh Brady was born in Pennsylvania and enlisted in the US Army as an ensign in 1792 and served in the western expedition under General Anthony Wayne, which culminated in the Battle of Fallen Timbers. A captain by 1799, he was appointed a colonel of the 22nd Infantry in 1812 and led his troops at the battle of Chippewa, displaying great bravery. Later he was wounded at the battles of Lundy's Lane and Niagara. He was retained in the Army reorganization of 1815, becoming colonel of the 2nd Infantry and in 1835 was placed in command of the northern department, of which Detroit was the headquarters. He kept peace on the border during the Patriot War and was brevetted major general for faithful service in 1848. He was killed by a fall from his horse in Detroit in 1851.

April, 1837, the state purchased the Detroit & St. Joseph Railroad and renamed it the Michigan Central. The following year, its tracks reached Ypsilanti and the main depot in Detroit was constructed at Michigan and Griswold Street. The fare to Ypsilanti was $1.50, with two trains running daily.

A canal was to be dug from Mt. Clemens on the Clinton River to the mouth of the Kalamazoo and another was to link the Saginaw River with the Maple, a tributary of the Grand River. Yet another was to be dug around the falls of the St. Mary River between Lakes Superior and Huron. Construction began on the Clinton-Kalamazoo Canal in 1838, with a ceremonial ground-breaking by Governor Mason. This canal would extend 12 miles along its proposed route before building stopped in 1843.

In the midst of all this speculation, potential project, and panic, an international situation arose involving Michigan and Canada. In December, 1837, revolts against the proper authorities broke out in Upper and Lower Canada (Ontario and Quebec, respectively). Known as the Patriot War or the Rebellion of 1837, it was an attempt by the French in Lower Canada to gain independence and the British in Upper

Canada to remove from power a selfish ruling group known as the Family Compact. This compact consisted of leading members of the government of Upper Canada (present-day Ontario) who shared several things, including religion, social background, connection by marriage, undying support for the Church of England and the unwavering belief that the province must always be a British possession. Controlling both houses of parliament in Canada, they hated all things American, especially popular democracy.

Many people in the United States sympathized with the rebels, seeing them in the same light as those most recently in Texas who overthrew their Mexican rulers in 1836. Many Americans saw this rebellion as the beginning of the end of British domination in North America.

Shortly after the outbreak of hostilities, the US department of state requested Governor Mason to arrest all those participating in hostile demonstrations against the British government. As a warning to all concerned, the governor issued a proclamation reminding American citizens of the neutrality laws.

Supporters of the rebel cause made up a small percentage of Michigan's population, but they were still too numerous for the governor to arrest. On January 1, 1838, they held a mass meeting in Detroit and collected funds for the Patriots. Five days later, a group of them broke into the Detroit jail and stole 450 stands of firearms that the militia had moved there for safekeeping. They then seized the schooner *Ann*, tied up at a wharf, loaded her up with the muskets, cannon, and about 130 men, and sailed for Gibraltar, where they prepared to invade Canada.

It was the responsibility of the US government to prevent an attack on a friendly nation and General Hugh Brady, commander of the Lakes District, knew his duty. Headquartered in Detroit with no real troops in or near the city, the US district attorney asked Governor Mason for help in taking the *Ann* into custody.

The governor called out the militia and, because their arms were stolen from the jail, marched them to the US arsenal at Dearbornville and equipped them with federal-owned arms. They marched back to Detroit and boarded two ships, sailing for Gibraltar on January 8, 1838. When they arrived, the rebels had already left for Canada.

Bitter complaints from the British and Canadian governments over the non-use of military force to disperse the rebels resulted in the stationing of three companies of regulars in the area by late January. In spite of the presence of these troops, the Patriots attempted another invasion of Canada.

On February 24, they crossed the Detroit River on the ice to Fighting Island in Canadian waters. Learning this news, General Brady led his troops downriver and stationed them opposite the island with orders to arrest any armed men on their way to and from the island. The British commander then threatened to chase the rebels into American territory. Brady ordered markers set up to define the boundary line and promised to repulse any invasion of American territory by British troops. The next day, the British opened up with artillery on the Patriots' position. Upon the British advance, they broke and fled to the Michigan shore where they were disarmed and arrested.

Trouble on the border broke out anew in December, 1838. General Brady dispersed a group of Patriots east of Detroit and disarmed them. Undaunted by this reverse, a company of them seized the steamer *Champlain* at a Detroit wharf early on the morning of December 4. They sailed for Canada and landed above Windsor. Surprising the troops at the Windsor Barracks, they captured most of them and set fire to the building. They then started for Sandwich. On the road, they met an army surgeon, Dr. J.J. Hume, and killed him. Upon hearing of the murder, British Colonel John Prince ordered four prisoners that his militia had in hand executed by firing squad. This force, combined with regular troops from Fort Malden, routed the Patriots completely, killing or capturing most of them. The Battle of Windsor was the last engagement of the rebellion.

One of the results of the Patriot War was the construction of the first iron warship on the Upper Great Lakes. Launched during the summer of 1844, the *USS Michigan* was of 500-tons burden, mounted with two eight-inch guns and four 32-pounders. She remained in service as a training ship until 1923.

Another result was the authorization to build Fort Wayne in 1841. Built on the Detroit River at the foot of Livernois Avenue, it was completed in 1851. A square-bastioned fortress with barracks built of stone, it never fired a shot in anger.

Fort Wayne

In 1840 at the point of the Detroit River closest to British Canada, the US Army began surveying land for the placement of an artillery post. The five-point star fort was Detroit's third and the first built by the Americans and was slated to have the most up to date cannon capable of firing on the Canadian shore. Following the Patriot War, the United States began planning new forts for border defense from the east coast to the Minnesota territory and the Detroit fort was named after General Anthony Wayne, the victor at Fallen Timbers over the Native Americans. Before any cannons were installed, diplomacy intervened, and Britain and the United States signed a treaty to settle any boundary disputes diplomatically. Fort Wayne was re-commissioned as an infantry post and served the Army through the Vietnam War as an induction center.

EXPLOITING NATURAL RESOURCES

In the midst of the painful grip of financial panic, the Whig Party in Michigan saw their opportunity to gain control of the state government. Meeting in Marshall in the fall of 1839, the party convention blamed all of the current problems on Governor Mason and the Democrats. They then nominated William Woodbridge of Detroit for governor.

Woodbridge was anything but a typical politician. He was a stern, retiring scholar from Ohio who came to Michigan as secretary of the territory in 1814. But he was ambitious for office, having served as territorial delegate to Congress and judge of Michigan's supreme court. People looked to him for his honesty and strength of character.

Governor Mason by this time had no desire to run again, which coincided with the feelings of his party's conservative element. They saw him as a liability and nominated Elon Farnsworth in his place.

The outcome of the election was never in doubt. The radical Democrats would have nothing to do with Farnsworth and supported the Whig ticket, along with hundreds of other voters who blamed the Democrats for the Panic of 1837. The Whigs promised sweeping reforms.

Woodbridge won and the Whigs controlled both houses of the legislature.

In the autumn of 1841, Stevens T. Mason, lamenting his fall from favor, moved to New York City and began to practice law there. He died on January 4, 1843, at the age of 31. Among the many important acts that Mason pushed through the first state legislature are two that should be mentioned here. The first detailed an ambitious internal state improvement plan involving roads and canals but failed for lack of proper financing. The second created the Comprehensive State Education Plan, which provided for the organization of common schools. Rev. John D. Pierce, first superintendent of public education, organized a system that included primary schools, a university, and branches of the university to service intermediate schools. All education was to be free and supported by taxes, with some financial assistance from the state. Free schools did not come at once, but the ideal was eventually reached.

The US Congress gave the 16th section of each township to the state for the benefit of all schools. These sections were given to the superintendent of public instruction and proceeds from their sale were placed into the primary school fund. Interest on the money was then distributed to school districts.

The legislature selected Ann Arbor as the site of the state university, primarily because a local land company offered 40 acres free of charge. The university was to have three departments: the arts, law and medicine, and literature and science. A Board of Regents was to be the governing body, and 72 sections of land were sold for $547,000 to provide financing. The University of Michigan opened in the fall of 1841 with two professors and six students.

The Lumber Boom

With the exception of numerous prairies and oak openings, Michigan was densely wooded. The primary species of tree was pine in three varieties: White, Norway, and Jack. They stood about 125 feet tall and rose 100 feet before the branches began. Some 6,000 square miles of pineland grew adjacent to water routes in the Lower Peninsula alone, making the pine affordable to harvest, as the greatest cost in this early industry was transportation. There would be

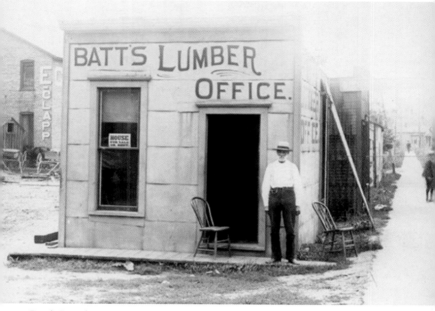

Batt's Lumber Office, corner South Madison and River Street, circa
1884, Monroe
Willard Library

more money made in Michigan lumber than in California
throughout the gold rush.

The need for this lumber came slowly as it was directly
proportionate to the course of settlement in Michigan; the
more settlers, the greater the need for finished lumber. As
towns were established along water routes, so too were
sawmills; the early mills were water powered. Detroit
records indicate the operation of mills as early as the 1740s
located on the Black, Pine, and St. Clair Rivers, in what
would become lower St. Clair County in the pine region
most accessible to town. Logging and lumbering would
move from there to Port Huron, Flint, and finally Saginaw
by the 1830s.

Saginaw had a steam sawmill in 1834, built by Harry
Williams and his nephews, who were agents for the
American Fur Company. The decline of the fur business
made the decision to enter lumbering easier and these men
remained to become founders of the industry that was to
make Saginaw famous.

Historic Mill Creek

One of the oldest industrial sites in the Midwest is Mill Creek, established in 1779 in response to British governor Patrick Sinclair's need to have boards to build a new fort and town on Mackinac Island. Robert Campbell built a sawmill on this site, powered by the falling waters of the creek. The complex later included a grist mill, an orchard, a blacksmith shop, a warehouse, and several homes. It continued as a sawmill until 1839, was acquired by the Mackinac Island State Park in 1975, and opened as a working sawmill once again in 1984.

There were other pioneer lumbermen in the region as well. Albert Miller, a probate judge, built a mill at Portsmouth near the mouth of the Saginaw River in 1836; George Hazelton and Charles Merrill had mills on the Flint River in 1840; the village of Lower Saginaw had a mill in 1847—ten years later, objecting to the word "Lower," citizens would rename the place Bay City. By 1860 there were more than 70 mills on the Saginaw River and its tributaries, producing over 131 million board feet of lumber. Saginaw was the first great center of the Michigan lumber industry.

The western side of Michigan also saw the development of the lumber industry, albeit at a smaller pace. In 1832 Pierce Barber built his sawmill at Paw Paw, Michigan, along the river of the same name, which the Native Americans named after the paw paw fruit growing along its banks. It was here that Charles Mears and his two brothers, Massachusetts natives, opened their store in 1836. The following year, they built a mill on the southeast shore of White Lake. Knowing that he needed a market, Mears had a sloop built at St. Joseph in 1838 and sent a cargo to Chicago that same year.

Steadily expanding his activities, Mears built another mill on Duck Lake, just south of White Lake in 1844, and in 1849 a third on Black Creek, just above Pere Marquette, now Ludington. Mears later became a state senator.

The first sawmill on the Muskegon River began to operate in 1838, and there were three mills running on Muskegon Lake by 1840. Some of the early operators were John Ruddiman, Theodore Newells, Martin Ryerson, and Henry Knickerbocker. Delos A. Blodgett was also rising to success during this period. By 1860 Muskegon was producing over 75 million board feet of lumber, the largest output on the west coast of Michigan.

Perhaps the man who left an indelible mark on the area was Charles Hackley, who arrived in Michigan in 1856 with seven dollars to his name. At his death in 1906, his estate was reportedly worth more than $12 million. Unlike some of the lumbermen who took their wealth and left the state, Hackley donated more than $6 million to the city of Muskegon, saying that, "a rich man... owes his fortune to the public. He makes money largely through the labor of his employees..." His money went to a hospital, an art museum, schools, churches, a park, and a library. Hackley Park remains a city-center jewel, with its Civil War Soldiers monument and statues donated by the namesake.

On the Manistee River, John Stronach and his sons built the first mill in 1841. In 1845 Joseph Stronach built a steam mill on Manistee Lake, followed soon by others. Logging in the Grand Traverse area began in 1847 when William Boardman of Napierville, Illinois, bought land on a stream running through present-day Traverse City. His son, Horace, began logging there that same year.

Lumbering in the Upper Peninsula was in its infancy at this time, with just a few mills providing local lumber needs. Daniel Wells, Jr., and Jefferson Sinclair built a mill at Escanaba in 1846 and were joined by Nelson Ludington in 1848. Mills on the Menominee River, which was to become the greatest carrier of logs, were built in the 1840s, at first on the Wisconsin side.

Statistics for the lumber industry for the period of 1840 to 1860 are impressive for a new business but would later be surpassed. In 1840 there were 500 mills in operation; by 1860, 1,000. The value of this wood grew from $1,000,000 in 1840 to $6,000,000 in 1860, with nearly 8,000 million board feet sawed.

MINERAL WEALTH

From their earliest explorations, white men knew there was copper in the Upper Peninsula, a fact, as has been shown, that Native American had known since prehistoric times. Attempts at mining during the 18th century were unrewarding and abandoned on the Ontonagon River. Governor Cass' expedition and the subsequent published report renewed interest in the mineral.

In 1837 Cass appointed Douglas Houghton the first state geologist. Houghton immediately undertook a survey of the mineral resources of the state. He made his report in 1841, stating that there were deposits of iron, lead, silver, copper, and other minerals in the Upper Peninsula. He expressed his belief that copper was the only mineral that could be profitably produced but changed his opinion three years later upon the discovery of vast quantities of iron ore at or near the surface in the area of present-day Negaunee, Michigan. Extreme variations in the groups' compass needle precluded this discovery, so extreme that the compass was completely useless. Tragically, Dr. Houghton was drowned on October 14, 1845, when his boat capsized in a Lake Superior storm. He was 36 years old.

As a result of Houghton's report, men began entering the Upper Peninsula seeking copper. As early as 1842, Boston capitalists financed a project for working the veins of fissures near Keweenaw Point. Prospectors, speculators, and adventurers arrived in great numbers at Copper Harbor in 1845, two years after the place was named the headquarters of government agent Walter Cunningham, whose job it was to issue permits and leases for copper mines. The copper rush was on.

The influx of miners led politicians in Washington to believe that they needed protection from the Native Americans who still inhabited the area. Fort Wilkins, named for President John Tyler's Secretary of War William Wilkins, was built near Copper Harbor, between Lake Fanny Hooe and Lake Superior. General Hugh Brady, commanding the 4th Military Department, left Detroit with two companies of the 5th Infantry Regiment to begin construction of a stockade and barracks in 1844.

As it turned out, the Native Americans were friendly and a lot less dangerous than the miners when the liquor

Fort Wilkins

At the northern tip of the Keweenaw Peninsula along Lake Superior's shore stands the Fort Wilkins Historic Complex, a well-preserved 19th century fort and lighthouse complex. Built in 1844 to keep the peace between miners and Native Americans during Michigan's copper boom, the post was abandoned just two years later, then very briefly re-garrisoned in the late 1860s. The setting is virtually undisturbed by modern intrusions and 19 buildings survive, 12 of them dating back to the 1840s. There are museum exhibits, costumed interpretations, and an annual Civil War encampment.

flowed. The garrison was ordered away in 1847, upon the beginning of the Mexican War. The fort was occupied only by caretakers until 1867 and vacated completely in 1870.

The copper country includes the Keweenaw Peninsula, Baraga County to the east, and Ontonagon County to the west. Among the most famous of the early mines were the Cliff mine, opened in 1845 at Keweenaw Point and closed in 1870; the Minnesota and National mines, opened in 1848 on the Ontonagon River (where the largest single mass of native copper, weighing nearly 500 tons, was found); the Quincy mines at Portage Lake, opened in 1848 and known for its sustained production (and the birth of the cities of Hancock and Houghton); the Pewabic lode, discovered in 1856; and the Calumet and Hecla, originally discovered in 1859 and destined to become the most famous copper mine in the world.

Almost 10 billion pounds of copper have been produced since 1845, generating more than $9.6 billion, 10 times more money than the California gold rush. Mining companies, not the individual prospector, profited from the copper mines. Some companies were fabulously successful and some were not. Copper employed thousands of immigrant workers, mostly miners from Sweden and the Cornwall region of Great Britain. It built cities and made millionaires. Its legacy can still be seen in abandoned mines,

Aerial view of Fort Wilkins in the fall.
Travel Michigan

ghost towns buried in the forest, and opulent architectural structures in cities across the region.

From the point where Dr. Houghton's compass failed, three major iron districts developed. They were the Marquette, the oldest and largest producer; the Menominee; and by the 1880s, the Gogebic districts. It wasn't long after news of the discovery became known that mining companies formed. In Jackson, Michigan, storekeeper Philo M. Everett and some of his friends formed the Jackson Mining Company in July, 1845. Originally intending to mine copper, Everett and three companions proceeded to Sault Ste. Marie, where they heard of a mountain of some kind of ore near Teal Lake.

Everett purchased a boat, hired a local pilot, and sailed to the mouth of the Carp River, where present-day Marquette now stands. Failing to find the heavy rocks, they sought out a local Chippewa chief, who readily agreed to take them to the mineral. They traveled 12 or 13 miles through dense forest to Teal Lake and then south of the lake to the foot of a hill. There lay a tall pine tree that had been knocked down by a storm. Within the roots of this tree were many pieces of the rich iron ore they sought. The city of Negaunee (Chippewa for pioneer) was built on the site and has as its city seal an uprooted stump.

A little further on, Everett found a ridge of bare rock which he believed was a mountain of solid ore 150 feet high. He took some specimens of ore and sailed to Copper Harbor, where he entered his claim in the office of the government mineral agent. In 1847 the Jackson Mining Company began operations, breaking up the above-ground ore with sledge hammers and crow bars. The company built a forge in 1848 to smelt the iron, using charcoal for fuel made from hardwood trees. However, the high cost of supplies and transportation from the area kept the company in the red for a few years.

Another mining company founded Marquette and began mining in 1849. Organizers of the Marquette Iron Company landed at the mouth of the Carp River and built some cabins and a forge. One of the workmen who accompanied them was Peter White, an ambitious 19-year-old from Detroit. White sailed on lake vessels and worked as a clerk on a lighthouse construction project and in stores in Detroit and Mackinac. In 1850 when the company opened a store at Marquette, he was put in charge. Three years later he started a bank and entered the state legislature in 1857; by 1860 he was an influential person and continuing to grow in reputation.

A third company, the Cleveland Iron Company, was organized in 1847 by 15 men, including a young lawyer and a physician. Claiming the same piece of land as the Marquette Iron Company, the Cleveland group proved earlier occupancy, appealed to the US government, and won. In 1853 they began operations, facing the same difficulties as the others. To solve the problem of transportation, they built a plank road from Ishpeming to Marquette in 1855. It wasn't until 1857 when a steam railroad was constructed that the mining become more profitable. The ore was unloaded on the docks at Marquette, then hauled aboard ship in wheelbarrows, a slow and expensive process. In 1859 the Cleveland Company built a new dock reaching 400 feet into the harbor. On this dock a high trestle with tracks for the mine cars was built, greatly facilitating the shipment of iron ore to the lower Great Lakes.

Ishpeming

First settled in 1854, Ishpeming was named in 1862 and its Native American name means "high place" or "heaven." Once the boom town of the Upper Peninsula during the iron ore mining era, the city boasted dozens of upscale stores and opera houses. There are two mines open to viewing: the Republic Open Pit Iron Mine and the Tilden Iron Mine. Ishpeming is the site of the US National Ski Hall of Fame and boasts as one of her notable sons John Voelker, author of *Anatomy of a Murder*, among other titles.

THE "SOO" LOCKS

Part of the growing transportation problem in moving minerals and people by water was the rapids of the St. Mary's River between Lakes Superior and Huron. For some time people had been interested in a canal built around the rapids and William Burt surveyed the route. Difficulties with the US Army and the contractors led to the failure of the first attempt in 1839. Over the next decade or so, sailing and steam-driven vessels were actually dragged over the portage around the Sault.

The state petitioned the national government for financial assistance in building the canal. At first there was opposition in Congress due to ignorance of the need for a canal and the geography of the region. When no less a person than Senator Henry Clay said that "it is a work quite beyond the remotest settlement of the United States, if not in the moon," Michigan Senator John Norvell informed him otherwise. In 1852 Congress granted 750,000 acres of public land to the state to sell and help defray the cost of construction.

The western representative of the Fairbanks Scale Company of St. Johnsbury, Vermont, was summering at the Sault for health reasons when he heard the news of the land grant. Charles T. Harvey convinced his employers to take up the project. They in turn hired Detroit attorney James F. Joy to put a suitable bill through the Michigan legislature. The legislature passed the bill to seek bids for the canal in

February 1853, and two months later accepted the Fairbanks' bid. They organized the St. Mary's Falls Ship Canal Company to fulfill the terms of their contract with the state, which called for the canal to be completed in two years.

Charles Harvey was appointed agent in charge of operations by the company. He began by hiring men and buying horses, tools, and supplies and reached the Sault on June 1, 1853. Work began the very next day on this arduous project. They were miles from any source of supply and had to anticipate their every need. Shipping ceased early in the fall due to the weather, making it necessary to build warehouses to hold whatever they might need over the winter. Harvey also built shanties, a hospital, and mess halls for up to 1,600 men working on the canal.

Despite the dangers of winter that far north, work continued year-round and the canal was finished on time. Two locks—each 350 feet long, 70 feet wide, and 13 feet deep—raised and lowered ships from one lake to the other. The first vessels passed through in June, 1855.

The opening of the canal drastically reduced the costs incurred in shipping mining supplies and the minerals themselves to the manufacturing cities. Mine production greatly increased. The amount of iron ore shipped in 1855 was barely 1,500 tons. By 1860 it had risen to just over 114,000 tons. The shipment of copper increased from just under 6,000 pounds in 1855 to just under 12 million by 1860.

LAKE TRAFFIC

As the locks at Sault Ste. Marie linked Lake Superior to the rest of the Great Lakes system, shipbuilders stood ready to take advantage of the increased traffic. Steam ships were the great carriers of merchandise and of immigrants to the west. Three of the leading Michigan ship owners of this period were Oliver Newberry of Detroit and Captain Sam Ward of Marine City and his nephew, Eber Brock Ward. These men operated both sailing and steam vessels and their steamships were known for their luxurious passenger accommodations.

MICHIGAN'S NEW CAPITOL

The constitution of 1835 established the capitol at Detroit until the year 1847. Indeed, the capitol building at Jefferson

Avenue and Griswold Street had been in use since 1828. In 1847 the legislature was to find a permanent location for the seat of government. Detroit, Jackson, Marshall, and Ann Arbor all made great efforts to have it located in their town. Many legislators favored a more central location, believing in the future of the north country. Besides, choosing one of the site would definitely antagonize the others. In the midst of all this discussion came the offer of a grant of 20 acres of land in what was then Biddle City, in Ingham County, from landowner James Seymour. The offer included the erection of buildings as fine as those in Detroit. The site was literally in the wilderness with no railroads within miles but its location appealed to enough politicians and they voted to move the capitol there. They named the site Michigan, and for the first year its postmark read, "Michigan, Michigan." In the end, the name of the township in which it was located was chosen and since 1848 has been known as Lansing.

GROWTH AND PROGRESS

In the 25 years between Michigan's statehood and the Civil War, many foundations were laid for the development of the state. Michigan's natural resources were tapped; agriculture was developing as the Lower Peninsula was settled; the state's system of public education was established during this period; and immigration was increasing.

The largest recipient of the burgeoning economy was the city of Detroit. A cosmopolitan city of over 15,000 people in the 1840s, its population would explode to 21,000 in 1850, 41,000 in 1855, and 49,000 by 1860. It had quite an ethnic mix, with one in every seven foreign-born persons being Irish. It had an east side known as Germantown, a Jewish congregation, two African-American congregations, and a growing crop of Italian immigrants. Overall there were 50 churches in the city.

Detroit had several different factories, a large steam sawmill, three iron foundries, a brass foundry, and two breweries. The manufacture of tobacco began during this time and grew into a major industry.

The city had a Board of Education with 12 members, and by 1849 4,000 children were enrolled in 19 schools staffed with 21 teachers. Soon there would be a working telegraph and the streets illuminated by coal gas. Horse-

The Michigan State Fair

The country's oldest state fair was first held in 1849 in Detroit, and as was customary at the time it was held in a different city every year until 1905, when it settled permanently at the present fairgrounds at Eight Mile Road and Woodward Avenue. At the time the area was truly rural farmland, seven miles from Detroit's city hall. The land was purchased by Joseph L. Hudson of department store fame, and he donated the 135 acres to the Michigan State Agricultural Society on April 18, 1905.

drawn bus lines began running. The state legislature passed the Plank Road Act, allowing private companies to build roads and charge tolls. On the west side of Woodward, between Columbia and Vernor, the very first State Fair was held in September, 1849.

The Detroit River played an important role in the city's development as vessels of all types had to stop there going and coming through the lake system. New immigrants came in and natural resources went out, providing a need for more and more lake tonnage. Detroiters owned or had an investment in most of the ships in the district—383 in 1859, with a gross tonnage of 62,485. That same year, 3,065 ships passed up- and 3,121 down-river.

The Underground Railroad

Natural resources were not the only things passing through Detroit. Human cargo in the form of runaway slaves moved through the city to Canada and freedom on a clandestine system known as the Underground Railroad.

The vast majority of Michigan residents were opponents of slavery and made several organized attempts early on to form anti-slavery societies in the state. As this agitation grew, slavery opponents set up a secret system to aid fugitive slaves to reach free territory. Abolitionists followed regular routes with stations and two of the several main lines crossed Michigan. One, known as the Central Line, ran from Cass County through such communities as

The Underground Railroad

More than 40,000 fugitive slaves made their way to freedom through Detroit on the underground railroad. On October 20, 2001, a new monument was unveiled along the riverfront. Designed by African-American sculptor Ed Dwight, it is 11 feet high, 14 feet wide and seven feet deep. It depicts five black people looking across the river to Canada and freedom. Other sites include the statue of Laura Smith Haviland outside the Adrian City Hall. A Quaker, she kept runaways in her house and was so successful that a reward of $3,000 was put up for her capture. There is also the underground railroad monument in Battle Creek depicting Erastus Hussey, who with his wife Sarah helped more than 1,000 escaped slaves; the Dr. Nathan Thomas House in Schoolcraft—this couple helped as many as 1,500 fugitives; the Slave Room in Buchanan, which is actually a cave hidden behind a waterfall on the St. Joseph River; and the Second Baptist Church, the First Congregational Church, and St. John-St. Luke Evangelical Church, all in Detroit and used as way stations on the underground route.

"Underground railroad" station, 17 Calhoun Street, Battle Creek
Willard Library

Schoolcraft, Battle Creek, Marshall, Albion, Jackson, Grass Lake, Dexter, Ann Arbor, Ypsilanti, and Plymouth. From Plymouth, the "passengers" moved along the River Rouge to Detroit and across the Detroit River to Canada. The second line in the state ran through Adrian, Tecumseh, Saline, and Ypsilanti to Detroit and then to Canada.

THE KING OF BEAVER ISLAND

The moral and spiritual fervor of these years produced several religious sects. One of these was the Mormon Church, founded by Joseph Smith in Nauvoo, Illinois. One of the new converts to Mormonism was James Jesse Strang, who in 1844 was baptized and quickly became an elder of the Church. Later that same year Smith was assassinated while in jail for destroying a newspaper office critical of his teachings and church. Two elders immediately stepped up to take control, Strang and Brigham Young, both claiming to be chosen by Smith to succeed him. In the ensuing struggle for church supremacy, the followers broke into two camps: "Brighamites" and "Strangites," but Young won the struggle and immediately excommunicated Strang and soon after left with his followers for Utah.

Strang and his dissidents went to Spring Prairie, Wisconsin, where he tightened his hold on them, forbidding the eating of meat as well as material possessions and sexual immorality. As more non-Mormon settlers threatened their lifestyle, Strang led his growing flock to Beaver Island, located at the northern end of Lake Michigan and within Michigan's jurisdiction in June, 1848. They founded the city of Janus and on July 8, 1850, Strang proclaimed himself to be "King of the Kingdom of God on Earth" before 235 of his followers. He erected a large temple made of logs, owned a saw mill and a commercial boat, founded *The Northern Islander* newspaper, and published pamphlets and books on his faith and other subjects. As with all one-man-ruled groups, jealousies and enmities ensued and as such Strang was assassinated in 1856.

THE BIRTH OF THE REPUBLICAN PARTY

One of the several important historical events of this period had its roots in Michigan's anti-slavery movement. As part

Eber Brock Ward (1811-1875)

Eber Brock Ward is considered Detroit's first millionaire. Born in Canada, he started his career as a cabin boy on his uncle's sailing ship and later in life acquired timberlands, mining properties, and other businesses such as newspapers, railroads, lake ships, and a few banks to boot. In 1853 Ward acquired the Eureka Iron Works in Wyandotte and one of his many accomplishments is the turning out of the first Bessemer steel in the country.

of the Compromise of 1850, a more stringent Federal fugitive slave law was enacted, designed in part to derail the Underground Railroad.

Despite this act, the Railroad continued its operations in Michigan. The state legislature passed laws to protect the rights and liberties of the residents of Michigan, both black and white. Known as the Personal Liberty Laws, their chief provisions called for the prosecuting attorney in each county to protect and defend all persons claimed as fugitive slaves.

In 1854 Detroit merchant Zachariah Chandler helped organize political rallies in response to the Fugitive Slave Act. He was joined by attorney Jacob M. Howard and newspaperman Joseph Warren of the *Detroit Tribune*. A meeting held in Kalamazoo in June completed plans to hold a mass convention at Jackson on July 6. Ten thousand signatures were received in response to this call, which made it clear that there was a united front against the extension of slavery.

Some 1,500 people gathered under pleasant summer skies at Jackson on July 6, 1854. No hall was large enough to accommodate such a crowd, so they met in an oak grove outside of town. Chandler and Kinsley S. Bingham, a farmer, addressed the crowd, and the assemblage formed two committees, one on nominations and the other on resolutions. Lewis Clark, a fugitive slave, made some sincere statements (unrecorded though well received by the crowd) while the committee reports were being prepared. Lewis Clarke is said to be the original "George Harris" of

Fall view of the Sturgeon River near Gaylord
Gaylord Area Convention and Tourism Bureau

Harriet Beecher Stowe's "Uncle Tom's Cabin." Born a slave in Kentucky in 1815, Clarke made a successful escape sometime in the late 1830s and early 1840s and published a book entitled "Narratives of the Sufferings of Lewis Clarke" in 1845. Lewis and his brother Milton frequently gave lectures based on their experiences.

The most important resolution adopted here said that "we will cooperate and be known as Republicans until the contest is ended." But there were some brutal and bloody years to endure before that would happen.

6

MICHIGAN AND THE CIVIL WAR

Michigan's commitment to the Republican Party bore fruit with the election of Abraham Lincoln, whose victory was announced on November 10, 1860. On that day, the South Carolina legislature passed an ordinance of secession, soon followed by other southern states. Not until Lincoln took office were positive steps taken to crush the rebellion.

Michigan's political leaders advocated the preservation of the Union and close cooperation with the Lincoln administration. This policy was most effectively carried out by Zachariah Chandler, elected to the senate in 1857 and since then the state's leading political personality. Dominating the Republican Party, his abolitionist tendencies influenced national politics for decades.

Significant support to the Union cause was also given by Michigan Governor Austin Blair, elected in January, 1860, and remaining in office throughout the Civil War years. Blair, like Chandler, was affiliated with the anti-slavery movement, and his support of Lincoln's policies throughout the war were scarcely equaled by few of the war governors in the north. He recommended that the military power of the state be offered to the federal government.

The state legislature refused to repeal the Personal Liberty Bills, which protected the rights of African-Americans, and also passed a joint resolution that declared the supremacy of the federal government and recognized its full powers of self-protection and defense. They also pledged the military resources of the state to the national government.

Those resources were none too formidable at the time, since they consisted of only 28 independent militia companies with a total strength of 1,241 officers and men uniformed at their own expense, armed but poorly

Zachariah Chandler
(1813-1879)

Born in Bedford, New Hampshire, Chandler attended common schools and later taught in them before moving to Detroit in 1833. He became a successful merchant and began a political career by becoming mayor of Detroit in 1851. After an unsuccessful bid for governor as the Whig candidate in 1852, he was instrumental in the organization of the Republican Party in Jackson in 1854. Chandler was elected to the US Senate as a Republican in 1857 and served until 1875, when he was appointed secretary of the interior by President Grant. He was once again elected to the Senate in 1879 to fill a vacancy and served until his death in Chicago in November.

equipped, and with no regimental organization. The state spent a paltry $3,000 annually for their support, primarily because of indifference to the possibility of any war. The opening of hostilities would change all of that.

THE WAR BEGINS

On the evening of April 12, 1861, the manager of the Detroit Theater rushed onstage in the middle of production and announced that Fort Sumter, in the middle of Charleston Harbor, had been bombarded by southern forces. A stunned silence hung over the crowd, then the orchestra struck up "Yankee Doodle" and the audience rose and cheered the Union.

Not many people in Michigan were surprised that war had come. President Lincoln wasted no time in calling for 75,000 volunteers to preserve the Union. Michigan's quota called for one regiment of 1,000 officers and men. Governor Blair issued a formal call for 10 companies of the uniformed volunteer militia, which were already organized. A meeting in Detroit determined that the state needed $100,000 to equip and train them; it was decided to try and raise $50,000 in Detroit and an equal amount out of state. Twenty-three thousand dollars was pledged immediately,

Bohemes Orchestra, 1872–94
Monroe County Historical Commission

but the rest was hard to come by. The legislature came
through in May, authorizing the governor to raise 10
companies of volunteers and borrow the $100,000.

The 1st Michigan Infantry, or the "three months
regiment" as it was called, consisted of the following militia
companies recruited from the southeastern part of the state:
the Detroit Light Guard, Jackson Greys, Coldwater Cadets,
Manchester Union Guard, Steuban Guard, Michigan
Hussars, Burr Oak Guard, Ypsilanti Light Guard, Hardee
Cadets, and the Marshall Light Guard. Their colonel was
Orlando B. Willcox, a Detroit lawyer and West Point
graduate.

The regiment underwent vigorous training at Fort
Wayne and were mustered into federal service on May 2,
1861. On May 11, they marched to Campus Marti's,
opposite city hall, for a special ceremony. Thousands of
citizens crammed the common and watched as the ladies of
Detroit presented them their handmade flags. Two days

later, the unit boarded a steamer for the lake trip to Cleveland, their first stop on the way to Washington, DC.

"THANK GOD FOR MICHIGAN!"

On May 16, the regiment arrived at the nation's capitol, the first unit from a western state to do so. Shortly after, they were welcomed by the president, who was reported to say, "Thank God for Michigan!"

The regiment was assigned to duty around Washington, and the high level of their training (compared to the rest) enabled them to participate in one of the first actions of the war. They got their baptism of fire when they assisted in the capture of Alexandria, Virginia, just across the Potomac River. The regiment captured a troop of rebel cavalry (about 36 men), along with their horses and equipment, and took possession of a railroad depot. For the next two months, they would continue to occupy the town and patrol the surrounding countryside.

By July 1 about 80,000 Union soldiers were massed in and around Washington and were prepared to move disastrously forward to the Battle of Bull Run. The 1st Michigan, now brigaded with the 4th Michigan, recently arrived from its training camp at Adrian, Michigan, was ordered to march around the right side of the Union line and flank the Confederate position. After a long march under a broiling sun, these green troops ran right into a brigade commanded by General Stonewall Jackson, who had captured a Union artillery battery and were themselves about to turn the Union flank.

Crossing the Sudley Ford, the 1st advanced in good order, stopped, opened fire, and chased the enemy from the battery. The regiment found itself holding the extreme right of the Union line against three times their number. Turning obliquely to its left, the 1st charged no less than four times in an effort to stop the Confederates, taking more and more casualties. Their failure marked the end of the battle, and the entire Union army retreated in a panic toward Washington.

The 1st took an even 500 officers and men into the fight. They lost six, with another 37 wounded and 71 missing or captured, including Colonel Willcox. The *Detroit Free Press* said the "the action of the regiment all through the day was in the highest degree honorable, brave and gallant and reflects the greatest credit upon the state that furnished it."

HEROES ALL

The action of the 1st Michigan Infantry was indicative of the commitment, spirit, élan, and courage of the Michigan men (and in a few cases, women) who fought to preserve the Union.

Michigan contributed almost 90,000 to the Union army, of whom over 85,000 were volunteers. They came from all sections of the state and all walks of life. Attorneys, physicians, and schoolteachers answered the call to duty. They were poor as well as wealthy, of Irish, German, French-Canadian, English, Dutch, Scotch, American, Native American, and African-American heritage. They formed 31 regiments of infantry, 11 of cavalry, and single regiments of artillery, sharpshooters, colored troops, and engineers and mechanics. Over 600 men served in the Union navy. Michigan men fought in all of the major campaigns and battles of the war from First Bull Run in 1861 to the surrender of the last Confederate army in the West in 1865. Michigan served the longest, as the 1st Michigan Cavalry was finally mustered out of service in Salt Lake City, Utah, in 1866 after helping to put down an outbreak of Native American hostilities. Over 14,000 of them would pay the ultimate price to preserve the Union.

Within seven months of President Lincoln's first call for troops, Michigan sent forward 16,475 men, besides 13 companies attached to regiments from other states. They went to the front as 13 regiments of infantry, three of cavalry, and five batteries of artillery. By July, 1862, a total of 27,000 men—6,000 bodies beyond the state's quota—were in service, with five more infantry regiments and three artillery batteries being recruited from various parts of the state.

The first two infantry regiments were organized from existing militia companies from across the southern half of the Lower Peninsula, but the remainder of these early levies came from specific locations. The 3rd Michigan Infantry was recruited from the Grand Rapids area; the 4th from a number of counties on a line from Monroe to St. Joseph; the 5th and 9th from Wayne; and the 6th from Kalamazoo.

Flint, White Pigeon, and Niles were rendezvous points for the 10th, 11th, and 12th Regiments, while Kalamazoo and Grand Rapids contributed an additional regiment each.

Twice-Told Tales

The behavior of the 1st Michigan Infantry at Bull Run in July, 1861, would be indicative of the meritorious service of all Michigan troops in the war.

Overshadowed by the publicity surrounding the 1st Michigan was the service in the same campaign of the 2nd, 3rd and 4th Infantry Regiments. The 2nd was organized in late April, 1861, made up of militia companies not selected for service in the 1st. They were the Scott Guard of Detroit, Hudson Artillery, Battle Creek Artillery, Adrian Union Guard, Niles Color Company, Flint Union Greys, Constantine Union Guard, East Saginaw Guard, Kalamazoo Light Guard, and the Kalamazoo Blair Guard. Commanded by West Point graduate and Mexican War veteran Colonel Israel B. Richardson of Pontiac, they were engaged at Blackburn's Ford, Virginia, in the opening moves of the Bull Run campaign.

Recruited at the same time was the 3rd Regiment, organized at Grand Rapids but not mustered into federal service until mid-May, 1861. The 4th was mustered at Adrian and both units served together with the 2nd at Bull Run and throughout the ensuing Peninsula campaign in Virginia in 1862. They covered the Union retreat from the field at Bull Run and were among the last troops to arrive at Alexandria, Virginia, in fairly good order.

In active service at this time was the 7th Infantry, commanded by Colonel Norman J. Hall, a native of New York who spent his early years in Monroe. Hall was a West Pointer serving with the 4th US Artillery when in 1860 he was assigned to the 1st US Artillery, stationed at Fort Sumter. It can be said then that Michigan was represented from the opening guns of the war. After the fall of Sumter, Hall served on General George McClellan's staff when he was asked to command the 7th. The regiment distinguished itself at Antietam and Gettysburg but won everlasting glory at Fredericksburg on December 13, 1862.

Colonel Hall accepted the assignment to send a force across the Rappahannock River in boats to dislodge the rebels,

Israel Bush Richardson
(1815-1862)

Born in Vermont and descended from the Revolutionary War general Israel Putnam, Richardson graduated from West Point in 1841 and fought in the Seminole and Mexican Wars before resigning in 1855 to become a farmer in Michigan. At the beginning of the Civil War, Richardson recruited the 2nd Michigan Infantry Regiment and led a brigade at the first Battle of Bull Run. Promoted to brigadier general in August, 1861, he continued as brigade commander until the spring of 1862. As a major general, Richardson was wounded at Antietam by Confederate artillery. He survived until November, then died at army headquarters. Israel Richardson is buried in Pontiac.

who had been sniping at Union engineers attempting to build a pontoon bridge. They succeeded in driving out the enemy with heavy losses to themselves in killed and wounded. At the battle of Antietam, in Maryland, the 7th sustained losses of 70 percent, and at one point Hall himself rallied his troops by carrying the regimental flag. Again on the third day at Gettysburg and without waiting for orders, Hall moved his regiment forward to assist troops about to break under the pressure of Pickett's Charge.

Another Michigan infantry regiment that gained immortality at Gettysburg was the 24th, a unit organized in late 1862 from Detroit and Wayne County. It was a true cross-section of Detroit during this era. Of the 1,030 soldiers, there were 412 farmers, 88 laborers, 62 carpenters, 38 clerks, 34 sailors, 25 blacksmiths, and an assortment of printers, painters, masons, coopers, teamsters, students, butchers, millers, bookkeepers, bakers, tailors, and others. Commanded by Colonel Henry A. Morrow, a former judge in Detroit's Recorder's Court, the regiment was a member of the famed Iron Brigade. Along with Wisconsin and Indiana units, the brigade earned its nickname at Antietam. Baptized under fire at Fredericksburg, the 24th earned its acceptance into the Brigade for its coolness under fire.

Michigan at Gettysburg

In 1887 the Michigan legislature appropriated $20,000 for the erection of its monuments at Gettysburg. In the spring of 1889, the monuments were completed and are located as follows: 1st Infantry, between the Wheatfield and the Emmetsburg Road; 3rd Infantry, in the Peach Orchard; 4th Infantry, in the Wheatfield; 5th Infantry, in the woods west of the Wheatfield; 7th Infantry, near the Clump of Trees where Pickett charged; 16th Infantry and Sharpshooters, on Little Round Top; 24th Infantry, in McPherson's Woods; Battery I, on Cemetery Ridge; and, 1st, 5th, 6th and 7th Cavalry, east of town where the cavalry fight occurred.

Almost one third of the group was under 20 years of age; another 270 were 20 to 25; 193 were 25 to 30; almost one-tenth of the regiment were men 40 or older. Of all, 325 were foreign born, 357 were born in other states, and only 343 were native to Michigan.

As part of the 1st Corps, the Iron Brigade was the first in the line of march toward Gettysburg when the enemy was located. Frantic messages to bring up the infantry hurried the Iron Brigade's march to the sound of the guns. They began to deploy and the 24th found itself on the extreme left flank of the Union army. Out of breath after a hard run and pausing only to load their muskets, they charged into the flank of a Confederate brigade about three times their number. Supported by the 19th Indiana and 7th Wisconsin, they stunned the enemy, most of whom threw down their weapons and surrendered, including their commander.

Through the course of the day's fighting, the 24th Michigan was forced to change their position no less than six times, all the while under tremendous enemy fire. So many Confederates were on the field that individual regiments of the Iron Brigade were holding off entire rebel divisions until General George Meade could bring up the rest of his army.

As the Iron Brigade took up their sixth and final line of defense, the order came to withdraw. They had accomplished their mission and were able to withdraw to Culp's Hill and safety. Of the 496 men taken into battle that morning, only 180 remained. The 80 percent casualties suffered by the 24th was the highest of all Union regiments at Gettysburg. They gave better than they got, however. The capture of Archer's Brigade was a blow to the Confederates, always hard pressed for manpower. They also dealt the 26th North Carolina regiment the war's largest regimental loss—88.5 percent. They brought 800 men to the field and only 92 remained at day's end.

Although the 24th continued to serve admirably, the losses at Gettysburg ended its effectiveness as an elite fighting force. In February, 1865, it was ordered to Springfield, Illinois, and detached to guard draftees. The regiment's final task was an honorable one, as it was selected as an escort at the funeral of President Abraham Lincoln.

THE WESTERN THEATER

Michigan troops also served admirably in the western theater of the Civil War in the campaigns in Kentucky, Tennessee, Mississippi, and Georgia. Assigned to the Army of the Cumberland operating in Kentucky and Tennessee were a number of Michigan regiments of all types: the 9th, 10th, 11th, 13th, 19th, 21st and 22nd Infantry; the 2nd and 4th Cavalry; the 1st Engineers and Mechanics; and several artillery batteries. They served valiantly in a long list of campaigns and battles, especially Chickamauga, Chattanooga, Missionary Ridge, and Shiloh.

One soldier who could be held up as an example is Frank Baldwin. Born near Manchester and raised in Constantine, Michigan, Baldwin enlisted as a 20-year-old first lieutenant in the 19th Michigan Infantry in September of 1862. He was captured at the battle of Thompson's Station, Tennessee, in March of 1863 and later exchanged. As a captain, he joined General William Sherman's army in its campaign against Atlanta and the famous March to the Sea. At the battle of Peach Tree Creek, Georgia, on July 20, 1864, he became one of only 70 Michigan men to win the Congressional Medal of Honor during the Civil War. The citation reads, in part, "…under a galling fire ahead of his own men, and singly entered the enemy's line, capturing 2 commissioned officers, fully armed…"

Detroit skyline at night
Photodisc Green/Getty Images

troops to Cincinnati. On the train he met members of the 22nd, who eventually adopted him into the unit as a "mascot." At four feet tall and weighing a hefty 63 pounds, Clem had a uniform tailored to fit him and a drum small enough to carry, purchased by the men.

At the bloody battle of Shiloh, Tennessee, in September, 1862, Clem's lively spirit and drumming so impressed the officers and men of the regiment that they named him "Johnnie Shiloh." On May 1, 1863, he was officially entered onto the rolls of the 22nd as drummer boy

Electing to remain in the regular army after the Civil

for three years. One year later, Clem set aside his drum and carried a guidon (the regimental flag) to mark the formation line of the regiment. In the ensuing battle, he lost the guidon and managed to acquire a musket and ammunition. Clem and his company found themselves surrounded by rebels who demanded their surrender. His comrades escaped, but the boy was too slow. A Confederate colonel on horseback demanded his surrender and called him a Yankee devil to boot. Clem turned and shot the man from his horse, mortally wounding him. He hid until dark, then slipped back to Union lines and rejoined his regiment near Chattanooga, Tennessee. General Rosecrans promoted him to sergeant and assigned him to his headquarters staff. One month later, he was captured again and spent 63 days in a Confederate prison. Exchanged, Clem was an orderly sergeant on General Thomas's staff. Clem continued to see combat and was wounded at Atlanta while carrying dispatches. He was discharged in September, 1864.

THE STONEWALL REGIMENT

One of a few regiments to see active service in both theaters of war was the 17th Michigan Infantry. Rendezvoused at Detroit in May, 1862, the unit left for Washington in August and fought brilliantly at South Mountain and Antietam in September. In February, 1863, the regiment was transferred by railroad to Louisville, Kentucky, to the 9th Corps, then stationed near the Tennessee border. The corps was then ordered to Mississippi, where the 17th saw combat in the opening of the Vicksburg campaign. In August it returned again to Kentucky and moved into Tennessee at Knoxville. The unit had traveled some 2,100 miles in a single year, 1863. Not content with that achievement, the regiment was ordered back to Virginia for the opening campaign in 1864. There it remained, fighting with the army of the Potomac until the surrender.

THE MOUNTED ARM

In addition to 30 regiments of infantry, Michigan also furnished 11 regiments of cavalry, which were among the finest mounted units on the continent. One of their number would be among the very last troops to be discharged from service thousands of miles away from Michigan, almost one year after hostilities ceased.

George Armstrong Custer (1839-1876)

Born in New Rumley, Ohio, George Custer spent some of his early childhood years visiting his older sister in Monroe, Michigan. He graduated from West Point in June, 1861, and was assigned to duty as lieutenant in the 5th US Cavalry. His taste for action and gallantry had won him promotion and staff appointments when in June, 1863, he was promoted to brigadier-general and made commander of the Michigan Cavalry Brigade. Leading this brigade through some of the most important battles of the war, they captured 111 pieces of artillery, 65 battle flags and over 10,000 prisoners. Promoted to major-general, Custer was present at the surrender at Appomattox Court House. He and most of his 7th Cavalry Regiment were wiped out at the Battle of the Little Big Horn on June 25, 1876.

The 1st Michigan Cavalry Regiment was rendezvoused at Detroit under the direction of its colonel, Thornton F. Brodhead of Grosse Isle. It was mustered into service in September, 1861, and stayed in winter quarters in Maryland, undergoing training and performing picket duty for the army of the Potomac. Its officers and men were from different communities scattered across the breadth of the state. They were mounted on the best horseflesh Michigan could offer, as it was the state that had to furnish everything for a mounted regiment.

The 2nd Cavalry was organized at Grand Rapids by Congressman F.W. Kellogg in October, 1861, and soon after boarded the train for St. Louis, horses and all. They were probably the best armed unit in uniform, having received Colt revolvers and the Colt repeating rifle this early in the war. Something they didn't have, however, was a colonel. Shortly after their arrival in Mississippi, they fell under the command of one Gordon Granger. A West Point graduate and Mexican War hero, this active New Yorker was in command long enough to drill his troopers to a high state of efficiency and discipline. In March, 1862, Granger was promoted to brigadier general and again the regiment was without a commander. A commission was offered to another West Pointer, who jumped at the chance to lead a combat unit. The 2nd Michigan was not very impressed at its first glance of a short, bandy-legged, red-haired Irishman named Phil Sheridan.

The 2nd, idled due to the lack of a commanding officer, was in a near-mutinous state when Sheridan was appointed. That soon changed, as he led them on railroad breaking raids south of Corinth, Mississippi, behind enemy lines. The raids' success improved morale and the next undertaking would make a name for the regiment and Sheridan a general.

As the Confederates were withdrawing from the lines in Mississippi, the 2nd Michigan and 2nd Iowa, both under Sheridan's command, were ordered to follow and keep an eye on their movements. Confederate General P.G.T. Beauregard decided that Sheridan was a nuisance and ordered a full cavalry division, about 6,000 troopers, to clear him out of Booneville, where he was headquartered. The Michigan and Iowa men numbered just over 800 and many of them were sick.

The Confederates came in along the Buckland road, which entered town from the west, steadily pushing the Michigan pickets back. They drove in hard and were met by those Colt repeating rifles and dropped by the score. Never having experienced such a heavy volume of fire before, their Confederate commander, General J.R. Chalmers, was forced to change tactics, dividing his force to send it around Sheridan's left flank. There they ran into the 2nd Iowa, which was not as well armed. The situation was desperate and growing worse by the minute.

Sheridan rode back to camp and instructed Captain Russell A. Alger of Detroit to take two companies, about 90 men, along a back road until he was in the rebel rear. Then he was to turn up the Buckland Road and hit them from behind. The "ruse de guerre" worked. Chalmers' men panicked and broke, leaving about 125 men killed and wounded on the field and taking unknown numbers of wounded with them.

THE MICHIGAN CAVALRY BRIGADE

Perhaps the finest mounted organization in either army was the cavalry brigade composed of the 1st, 5th, 6th, and 7th Michigan Cavalry Regiments. The 1st, seen earlier, was an experienced unit when the brigade was formed in December, 1862, as part of the 3rd Cavalry Division of the Army of the Potomac.

On June 29, 1863, they received a new commander and together they would earn a reputation for recklessness, bravery, and élan—as well as their title, the "Wolverine Brigade." Newly promoted Brigadier General George A. Custer assumed command at the very beginning of a campaign that would culminate at Gettysburg, Pennsylvania.

It was on the last day at Gettysburg, July 3, 1863, when the Wolverine Brigade rendered its singular service to the Union cause. In the fields just east of the Union positions along Cemetery Ridge, they met the Confederate cavalry, under the command of General J.E.B. Stuart, in a headlong charge and prevented the encirclement and probable defeat of the Union army. The charge involved over 7,000 sabers on both sides. After Gettysburg, the brigade continued to see very active service, participating in raids and flanking movements until April, 1865, when men from the Michigan Cavalry Brigade received Lee's flag of truce, signaling the end of the war.

Their service was far from being over as the brigade was detailed to move west to fight Native Americans. The 5th, 6th, and 7th Regiments were finally mustered out of service at Fort Leavenworth, Kansas, by December, 1865. The 1st Cavalry did not leave service until March 10, 1866, at Salt Lake City, Utah.

COLORED TROOPS

In late July, 1863, the state of Michigan received authorization to raise one regiment of colored troops after much debate in Congress. The 1st Michigan Colored Infantry began recruiting on August 12, 1863, in Detroit under the direction of Colonel Henry Barns of Detroit. The regiment left its rendezvous on March 28, 1864, and joined the IX Army Corps at Annapolis, Maryland. Two weeks later it was sent to Hilton Head Island, South Carolina, as the 102nd US Colored Troops and was employed on picket duty.

Photo courtesy Michael Reed

Elmwood Cemetery

To walk through Elmwood cemetery is to walk through 150 years of history. Its residents live on in the names on many buildings, maps, streets, and history books. From early merchants to late mayors, the final resting place for Detroit and Michigan's famous is a place of peace and quiet. This near east side cemetery was the site of the Battle of Bloody Run where English soldiers were massacred during Pontiac's Rebellion in 1763. Among the 54,000 markers one will find "Maserati Rick" Carter, notorious drug dealer, buried in a $16,000 coffin with a Maserati grill; Helen Newberry Joy, the state's first licensed female driver, who drove her electric car from 1914 to 1958; John Blessed, one of the state's last stage coach drivers; Margaret Mather Findlayson, who rose from selling newspapers on Detroit street corners to become one of the world's leading Shakesperean actresses, most famous for her Juliet; and Count Cyril Petrovich Tolstoi, grandson of the great Russian novelist Leo Tolstoy, who wrote *War and Peace*.

A portion of the regiment was ordered to Jacksonville, Florida, for more picket duty and the destruction of railroads. It was here that the unit first came under fire from a force of rebel cavalry, which it easily repulsed, proving to its officers that its men could fight. Subsequent campaigning through eastern Florida hardened its resolve.

The regiment finally saw action as a unit at the Battle of Honey Hill, South Carolina, in November, 1864, and continued to be engaged in offensive operations throughout that state until late April, 1865. In its brief but honorable service, the 102nd lost 140 men to death and disease out of a total enrollment of 1,446.

THE HOME FRONT

The Civil War had a very profound effect on the state of Michigan. The ten-year period from 1860 to 1870 would see the state transformed into a national manufacturing powerhouse and a leading agricultural exporter.

The rush to arms beginning in 1861 disrupted the internal economy of the state by quickly draining its available manpower from the farms and cities. The state ranked eighth out of the 23 northern states in troops sent. This shortage left the work in the hands of older parents and wives, depressed farm prices, and left business weak in 1861. Weaker farms without sufficient manpower failed, while others scrimped by until the economy geared up to wartime levels.

There were three pieces of federal legislation passed in 1861 and 1862 that had both an immediate and long-term impact on Michigan: the Tariff Act of 1861, the Land Grant Act of 1862, and the Homestead Act of 1862. The latter act offered a 160-acre tract of land free to settlers who would reside on and develop the land over a five-year period. From January 1, 1863, to June 30, 1866, there were almost 6,000 entries for over 760,000 acres of Michigan land. In addition to this free land, the state land office sold more than 530,000 acres during the Civil War period. Improved acreage rose from 1.9 million to 3.4 million and tripled in cash value.

The labor shortage was somewhat alleviated by the influx of settlers to the state, both Americans and immigrants. Between 1860 and 1870, the population rose from 749,000 to 1,200,000, of which about 90,000 were immigrants. These people settled mostly on farms and in the agricultural industry and had a direct influence on industry throughout Michigan. All these new farms needed equipment, even if it was just an ax and a hoe. The older

farms as well had to be kept in operation. These factors plus the lack of manpower led to increased mechanization.

The McCormick reaper, built in Chicago since 1848, the Case thresher, built in Racine, Wisconsin, and John Deere's steel plow revolutionized farm work. The reaper alone could replace up to 20 men at harvest time. The production of wheat in Michigan almost doubled between 1860 and 1870, while at the same time early in the decade the harvest in Great Britain was below average. The states of the Midwest would emerge from this conflict as the granary of Europe.

The dairy industry also saw production of its products soar. In 10 years' time, the amount of butter produced rose

Winter at Old Presque Isle Lighthouse near Rogers City
Randall McCune

from 15,500,000 pounds to 24,400,000, and cheese from 1.6 million pounds to 2.4 million. Obviously, the number of cheese factories rose as well. Lenawee County was first with 15 factories, producing 60 percent of the state's cheese.

The Civil War also brought prosperity to other parts of Michigan's economy. The Upper Peninsula's mining industry experienced the beginnings of a boom that would last for decades and propel the state into the lead in copper and iron production. In 1860 the Marquette range produced only 150,000 gross tons of iron ore and 5,000 tons of pig iron. By 1864 these figures jumped to 248,000 gross tons of ore and 12,951 tons of pig iron.

Similar developments took place in the copper industry. At first the domestic market was sluggish, but war demands made Michigan copper the main source for ore. Prosperity hit the mining communities of Houghton, Hancock, Eagle Harbor, Portage, Ontonagon, and Rockland as the price of copper soared from 19 cents per pound in 1861 to 43 cents in 1865.

Of the 20,000 people inhabiting the Upper Peninsula, some 1,500 men enlisted to fight in the army, creating a potential labor shortage in the mines. In response, mine operators sent agents to Northern Europe to hire miners, and the companies paid $90,000 to bring them to the Keweenaw Peninsula. Hundreds of Swedes responded and became the advance party of the Scandinavian migration to the area.

The increased demand for goods also brought prosperity to manufacturing in the Lower Peninsula. The manufacture of clothing, boots and shoes, hats and caps, gloves and mittens, cutlery, and furniture increased significantly from 1860 to 1870. For example, the number of establishments producing clothing rose from 50 to 288 by 1870, boots and shoes from 282 to 765, and furniture from 131 to 246. These figures indicate that Michigan was becoming less dependant on products made in the home or imported from other states. Employment in these industries increased more than 100 percent during this time as well.

Specialized industries began to appear or increase in number and size during this decade. Hoop skirts and corsets were not produced in the state in 1860, but in the next 10 years there were 11 such firms employing 76 people. There were also no businesses canning fruits and preserves, vinegar, packing beef and pork, or producing flax, sorghum and tobacco in Michigan in 1860, yet each industry had at least five establishments by 1870.

The Land Grant Act of 1862

The other important piece of legislation that had a profound effect on Michigan was the Land Grant Act of 1862. This act set aside 30,000 acres of federal land to be given to the states for each member of Congress and used or sold for the support of education, basically providing for the establishment of one college in each state. Representative Justin Morrill of Vermont, sponsor of the bill, had as his model the Michigan Agricultural College, established in 1857, ten miles east of Lansing. Chronically short of funds, the college was greatly aided by the passage of this bill, which included stipulations for military training in its curriculum. It was one of the first institutions of its kind to provide for the scientific study of agriculture.

The Soldiers Return

While the troops were away fighting in the war, several institutions were established to provide for their families and themselves. With more money available during these years than ever before, charitable organizations assembled to provide support for soldier's dependants.

The Michigan Soldier's Relief Association, the Christian Commission, and the Ladies' Soldier's Aid Society were but three such groups that provided aid and relief to soldiers and their families. The Michigan Soldier's Relief Association claimed to be the first one in action and the last to leave. It started its work in the fall of 1861, collecting money and supplies to send to the front. They sent socks, underwear, canned fruit, newspapers, quilts, books, needles and thread, and anything else thought useful. The Christian Commission saw to the mental, spiritual, and bodily wants of the soldiers, while the Ladies' Aid Society saw to the needs of the sick and wounded.

On July 4, 1866, the last Michigan soldier was mustered out of service and returned home. Michigan had paid dearly for its part in the war. Out of 90,000 men, over 14,000, or about one in every six, were casualties. Approximately 10,000 of these men died from disease. More American soldiers lost their lives during the Civil War than in World War I, II, Korea, and Vietnam combined.

7

Corn, Furniture, Cherries, and Stoves

New Directions

The burgeoning agricultural and industrial activity during the Civil War did not stop with the Confederate surrender at Appomattox. The 30 years from 1866 to 1896 saw this activity grow and expand throughout the country and Michigan was no exception. Its lumbering, mining, and farming industries were in place and poised to take the state to greater heights as one of the nation's leading producers.

As Michigan's soldiers returned home to the grateful arms of their loved ones, plans surfaced to honor their sacrifices to the cause. Cities and towns across the state held parades as regiments marched in formation for the last time. The regimental flags, most of them shot through with holes from combat, were turned over to the state to be enshrined at the capitol.

Hundreds of communities planned monuments to the boys in blue, engraved with the names of those who served, living and dead, and erected in cemeteries and courthouse squares. Almost without exception, the local communities paid for these monuments through fund raising and subscriptions.

Soldiers' and Sailors' Monument

On June 20, 1861, after the war had hardly started and no major battles were yet fought, a group of concerned and patriotic citizens met in Detroit and resolved that a suitable monument should be erected to the memory of those who died in defense of the Union. The group set up a committee to carry out this plan, but set aside the work soon after that until the war's end.

Alphas Starkey Williams
(1810-1878)

Born in Deep River, Connecticut, Williams was left fatherless at the age of eight and motherless at the age of 17. He was, however, left with an estate of $75,000 which allowed him to graduate from Yale in 1831, study law, and travel, which he did extensively in the United States and Europe. Why he moved to Detroit is unclear, but he established himself as a lawyer and served as a probate judge, president of a bank, owner of a newspaper, postmaster, and member of the Board of Education. He enlisted in the local Detroit militia, the Brady Guards, in 1838 and worked his way up to major general 20 years later. Appointed a brigadier general in the regular army at the outbreak of the Civil War, Williams served with distinction throughout the conflict. A bronze statue was erected to him on Detroit's Belle Isle in 1921.

In 1865 the Michigan Soldiers' and Sailors' Monument Association organized and the project began anew. The association named individuals from all parts of the state to its board of directors and launched a campaign to raise $50,000 to finance the monument. Two years later, in 1867, it awarded a contract to build the monument to Randolph Rogers, an American sculptor and once a resident of Ann Arbor during the 1830s and 1840s. The monument was erected in Detroit's Campus Marti's, a gathering place of importance since 1805. On April 9, 1872, the seventh anniversary of the surrender, the monument was dedicated before 25,000 citizens crammed into Campus Marti's. Among those thousands, Generals Philip Sheridan, George Custer, and Alphas Williams were on the agenda along with the requisite number of politicians as speakers.

As Michigan's leading city, Detroit was to be the immediate beneficiary of the growth the state experienced during the war. In response to the government's needs, several industries got their start during this time. The Detroit Bridge and Iron Works was established in 1863 to replace those structures destroyed during the war. Two Detroit businessmen, James McMillan and John S. Newberry, organized the Michigan Car Company in 1864 to manufacture railroad freight cars on scale that would make Detroit one of the nation's leading producers of rolling stock. This led to the organization of numerous ironworks up and down the Detroit River, plenty to handle the ore production from the Upper Peninsula. The Eureka Iron and Steel Works, established at Wyandotte, was one of these. In 1864, the very first Bessemer steel was produced in the United States.

By 1870 the population of Detroit had reached nearly 80,000, with almost half of those foreign-born. The city occupied nearly 15 square miles and enjoyed free daily mail delivery. The Detroit Public Library opened its collection of 5,000 books to the public on the top floor of the old Capitol High School. African-American children were admitted to public schools for the first time and the state legislature created the Detroit Metropolitan Police Force.

Although the city did not have a single large factory, the two largest employed 700 men building railroad cars, and a number of other manufacturers had their start during this period. Jeremiah Dwyer organized the Detroit Stove Works. Returning Civil War veteran James Vernor found that his favorite concoction of ginger ale, left in an oak barrel, was delicious. Druggist Samuel Duffield and salesman Harvey Parke formed a partnership to sell pharmaceuticals. Taking on George Davis, they incorporated as Parke, Davis & Company and would become one of the nation's leading manufacturers of drugs and medicines. Dexter Ferry started up a seed business at this time, and William Davis received a patent for his "icebox on wheels," a refrigerator car used to ship fruits and fish by railroad.

The early stirrings of organized labor manifested in the organization of the Detroit Trades Assembly, a coalition of unions that boasted 5,000 members. Female taxpayers were given the right to vote for school trustees in 1867, but the state legislature balked at granting them total suffrage. At the same time the University of Michigan enrolled its first female students. The legislature did pass its first compulsory school attendance law in 1871 that required school children ages eight to 14 to attend school at least 12 weeks per year.

Other communities across the state had the same experience of founding industries, soon to be known worldwide. Grand Rapids and Kalamazoo were just two such places. In 1876 furniture manufacturers from Grand Rapids exhibited their products at the Centennial Exposition in Philadelphia. The responses brought buyers from across the country to the city to order more, and it wasn't long before the product was known everywhere. In fact, the popularity of Grand Rapids-made furniture prompted a federal court to rule that the words "Grand Rapids furniture" had acquired such a reputation that the American public understood that Grand Rapids furniture was "superior in design, workmanship and value to furniture purchased elsewhere."

The development of this city as a furniture center was due to the business talents of men such as William Heldane, A.B. and George Pullman, C.C. Comstock, A.D. Linn, and Z. Clark Twing. These last two gentlemen invented the dry kiln process for seasoning lumber, which drew the sap from the wood. The success of Grand Rapids furniture led other cities to establish similar factories. By 1890 Detroit had 20, and there were firms in Owosso, Muskegon, Big Rapids, Manistee, Saginaw, Holland, Allegan, Sturgis, Niles, Ann Arbor, Buchanan, Grand Ledge, and others.

But Grand Rapids had a number of other industries as well, such as factories producing freight cars, elevators, pumps, varnish, and tools.

THE GREAT FIRE OF 1871

One of the mottoes of the lumber industry at this time was "cut and get out," and with no thought for the future the industry created a tremendous amount of unused lumber. Loggers were paid so much per stump (pine) and the slashings from the trees and the smashed remains of trees rejected for one reason or another were left to rot on the ground. As this detritus dried out, it became an excellent fuel for a forest fire and fires would, from time to time, break out.

The most disastrous of all these fires took place in the fall of 1871. The summer had been unusually hot and dry and the forest brush was like tinder. On Sunday, October 8, the famous Chicago fire broke out and only died down two days later after wiping out the entire city. As the fire raged in Chicago, a southwest gale of tornado proportions sprang up. Old timers asserted that wind carried sparks from this fire across the lake into Michigan. It may be true or not but fires broke out all along the west coast of the state.

Men from Holland, Michigan, were fighting small fires in the woods near town when a high wind rose and spread the flames. In two hours the entire town was destroyed with only one person dead but 300 families left homeless. Farther north up the shore of Lake Michigan, Manistee was also a fire victim with half of the town completely destroyed. From the western shore, flames driven by strong winds swept across the Lower Peninsula, laying waste to everything in its sight in Lake, Osceola, Isabella, Midland, Saginaw, Tuscola, Sanilac, and Huron Counties. Some 18,000 persons were left homeless. Relief committees appointed by Governor Henry P. Baldwin aided the destitute. Instead of sending money to Chicago, the people of Michigan turned to help their own.

SALT OF THE EARTH

Another of the industries that benefited from lumber was the salt industry. Underneath the soil of the state lay immense quantities of rock salt and brine. Douglas Houghton found salt springs in the Saginaw region and made efforts to produce this slat commercially in the 1850s, though was unsuccessful due to the process being slow and expensive. For motivation the state legislature offered a bounty for the manufacture of salt to any company reaching a 5,000 bushel output. Enter the lumberman. Using the scrap wood of the sawmills as fuel to evaporate the brine, production costs dropped. Soon after, the Saginaw valley was full of salt wells. It wasn't long before a better method was found. Using exhaust steam from the mills to drive off the brine sent costs down to 40 cents a barrel by 1879. The next year Michigan produced nearly 2.5 million barrels, which amounted to half of the salt in the nation. Salt followed lumber as the latter moved westward, and plants were established at Manistee, Ludington, and Frankfort. When the lumber eventually faded out, the manufacture of salt became even more important in these areas.

Detroit's Salt Mines

A ghostly city with its own network of highways lies deep beneath the city of Detroit. 1,200 feet below the surface and spread out for more than 1,400 acres lies a gigantic salt mine, begun in 1896. This salt bed extends for over 170,000 square miles under Michigan, Ohio, Ontario, Pennsylvania, New York, and West Virginia. The International Salt Company operated the mine from 1907 to 1983, when costs forced the company to shut down operations.

The salt industry also moved southward from the Saginaw valley along the St. Clair and Detroit Rivers. The presence of a deep vein of rock salt in the vicinity of Detroit had been known for a long time, but the first use of it was in the making of soda ash. A well was sunk near Wyandotte to provide the salt needed to make the soda ash necessary for the manufacture of glass. As methods improved, by-products and auxiliary businesses of the salt industry would overshadow the original business.

LUMBER BOOM

The period from 1860 to 1890 saw an enormous increase in Michigan of lumber production. Loggers moved northward and inward and made use of every stream in the Lower Peninsula. Production in the Upper Peninsula added millions of board feet to the output of the state, which peaked in 1888 when 4,292,000,000 board feet of lumber was sawed, worth probably in excess of three billion dollars. That does not include millions of shingles, staves, pickets, railroad ties, and squared timbers that were produced. The years after 1888 saw a steady decline, but Michigan led the nation in lumber well into the next century.

This great lumbering boom did not materialize until the white pine sources of Maine and other states had been depleted. At the same time there was a growing demand for it in the prairie states whose source of supply, Chicago, was the link to Michigan sawmills. By 1890 there were 2,000 sawmills in Michigan employing over 25,000 people.

On the Lake Huron side of the state, logging continued in the regions that had been opened earlier. Production in the Saginaw Valley increased enormously, as experienced Eastern operators moved in, extending their holdings of land and cuttings of timber. The immediate area had a water system available as the Tittabawasee, Shiawasee, Cass, Flint, Pine, and Chippewa Rivers all flowed into the Saginaw River. As the industry moved beyond this system, narrow gauge railroads were built to haul timber to the water. During the 1870s the Flint and Pere Marquette, the Saginaw and St. Louis, and the Jackson, Lansing and Saginaw Railroads helped load the millponds with logs year-round. Towns situated near the railroad and river became important lumber centers. For example, in 1873 the town Midland, on the Pere Marquette Railroad and the Tittabawasee River, owed its importance to its 27 mills.

Important operators in the Saginaw region at this time were Jesse Hoyt, David Whitney, C.F. Marston, and Henry Howland Crapo. The future lumber barons would put their fortunes to good use in philanthropy and public office: Crapo would take his seat as governor in 1865 and Whitney would support the arts in Detroit. Because of the demand for ships to transport the lumber to market, Saginaw and Bay City became important shipbuilding centers on the eastern side of Michigan.

David Whitney came to Detroit from his native Massachusetts in 1859. The 29-year-old started a lumber business with his brother, Charles. When they dissolved the profitable partnership in 1877, David used his money to buy pine lands, both in Michigan and Wisconsin. Paying from three to 50 dollars an acre, he bought hundreds of thousands of acres and made profits sometimes 100 times his original cost.

He put his instincts for land values to good use in Detroit and became known as "Mr. Woodward Avenue," buying up properties along this strip as the city developed northward from the river. In 1890 he built the five-story Grand Circus Park Building. Upon his death in 1900, Whitney had a fortune estimated at $15 million, making him the wealthiest man in Detroit at that time.

Another native of Massachusetts in 1856 was Henry H. Crapo, who moved to Flint, Michigan, at the age of 52, due primarily to investments in pine lands. Lumber made his fortune. In 1861 he was elected mayor of Flint, and in 1862 he was the state senator from Genessee County. In 1864 he was nominated on the Republican ticket for governor and won election by a large majority. He was reelected in 1866 and held office until his retirement in January, 1869. After his death in July of that same year, the Detroit Tribune said that he "showed himself to be a capable, discreet, vigilant, and industrious officer."

Moving northward, mills were built at Tawas City, Oscoda, Harrisville, Ossineke, Alpena, and Cheboygan. The Au Sable River was the main waterway, carrying a tremendous amount of logs to Oscoda. Alpena, at the mouth of the Thunder Bay River, became an important mill town. One of the earliest lumbermen, George N. Fletcher, built his mill and helped lay out the village, initially called Fremont, in 1856. Together with his sons, he remained one of the biggest producers. Others at Alpena included F.W. Gilchrist and Albert Pack. Alpena's largest amount of lumber was cut in 1888—215,000,000 board feet. Cheboygan reached its peak of production later than the town to its south. In 1873, 41,000,000 feet were cut and hit a high mark in 1890 of 127,540,000 feet.

On the west coast of Michigan, the industry's movement and development was similar. The Grand River and the Kalamazoo were early carriers of logs and were the first to decline due to the larger stands of pine farther north. Grand Rapids reached its peak production in 1873 with 56,000,000 feet and was left with hardwoods after that, which led to the development of the furniture capitol.

Allegan and Kalamazoo began to manufacture paper from wood pulp before 1890 as a result of the pine being run out. The principle center was Grand Haven, situated on Lake Michigan at the mouth of the Grand River. There, the two largest producers were Gilbert and Sons and William M. Ferry and Sons, sawing their largest output, 192,000,000 feet in 1882.

The largest production of any city in Michigan was at Muskegon, where the number of mills increased yearly. In 1873, they cut 329,689,000 board feet, which more than doubled to 665,449,000 feet in 1887, the peak year. C.H. Hackley & Co., McGraft and Montgomery, Tillotson and

David Whitney Jr. (1830–1900) at Home

David Whitney Jr. was one of the wealthiest lumber barons in the Midwest. He left a prime example of residential architecture in his Detroit residence, which is currently operated as a fine restaurant. Construction began in 1890, taking four years to complete. The building's exterior is made of pink jasper, mined in South Dakota. The luxurious interior is reminiscent of Napoleonic Paris and its features include silk-covered walls and ceilings, tapestries, extensive woodwork, leaded crystal, and Tiffany windows. The 21,000-square-foot home has 52 rooms, 10 bathrooms, 218 windows, 20 fireplaces, an elevator, and a secret vault in the original dining room. Some say the place is haunted, probably by Whitney himself, as there have been incidents of chairs moving by themselves and tables vibrating.

Blodgett, Mann and Moon, and Ryerson, Hills and Co. were the prominent mill operators there.

Next to Muskegon, Manistee was the greatest producer of lumber on the west coast. The water system, made up of the Manistee River and its tributaries, flowed through eight counties and some of the best pine country in the state. Millions of logs were sent to the mills on Manistee Lake, which produced 300,000,000 board feet in 1892. One of the principle lumbermen in the area was Louis Sands, a Swedish immigrant who began as a laborer in 1853. Saving enough money to begin taking small logging contracts, Sands quickly expanded his operations and acquired land on Manistee Lake and the Manistee River in 1878. He built ships to carry his lumber to market and ran a narrow gauge railroad to bring out the logs. In 1879 salt beds were discovered under Manistee and Sands was among the first to manufacture the salt. He also owned a bank, gasworks, and electric plant in Manistee.

The forests of the Upper Peninsula contributed their share to Michigan's lumber wealth. The principle lumber

City Bank, 1913, Battle Creek
Willard Library

center was Menominee, which had its first sawmill in 1836, soon followed by many others.

Another large center of production was Escanaba, in Delta County, where the North Ludington Company was the dominant firm. On the Ford River not far from the town, the Ford River Lumber Company had a large mill. In Schoolcraft County, Manistique had mills owned by the Chicago Lumber Company. A number of other towns such as Baraga, Dollarville, Grand Marais, Munising, and Ontonagon also produced lumber for export. The Chicago and Northwestern Railroad linked these points together by the early 1870s and also handled the transportation of ores to shipment points on the Great Lakes.

AGRICULTURE

As the lumbermen made more and more trees disappear, farmers moved into the middle to northern counties in the Lower Peninsula. Between 1860 and 1890 farming became a great industry. Prior to this time, farmers grew crops to supply their own families and sold surpluses, if any, in the immediate area. The clearing and cultivation of more land meant larger crops and bigger surpluses. The numerous railroads in the state provided the means to ship produce to distant markets, and farmers who lived near or who could send produce to a lake port had the luxury of cheaper shipping costs.

By 1879 agricultural products accounted for approximately one-half of the income derived from all of the natural products of the state. In 1850 there were almost 2 million acres of improved land and just over 34,000 farms found mostly in the four southern tiers of Michigan counties. By 1881 the farms numbered just under 120,000 and contained over 6 million acres of cultivated land. The onrush of settlers to the northern counties practically doubled the amount of land under cultivation.

The largest Michigan farm crop and the most valuable was wheat. The average number of bushels per acre in 1871 was 19, which resulted in a return of $23 per acre. The wheat exported from Michigan brought more money to the farmers than the total of all other surplus crops combined. All the counties in Michigan shared in wheat production.

Corn, oats, barley, buckwheat, clover, potatoes, hay, and hops were also cultivated extensively. Beets, turnips, carrots, and other garden vegetables returned good yields, both below and above the Straits of Mackinac, although the Upper Peninsula farmers and gardeners from the northern countries were more successful.

Because of the glaciers that covered the state, Michigan has a great variety of soils. Farmers began to learn that special crops would thrive on what had been considered waste land. For example, when drained, swamps could provide a deep rich soil for celery, cranberries, and peppermint. Before 1890 Michigan was producing more peppermint oil than all of the other states combined. Celery became a substantial cash crop with Kalamazoo as the principle center of celery production by 1890. With up to three crops a year, at the height of the season daily exports of between 30 and 40 tons shipped from Kalamazoo. Newberry, in the Upper Peninsula, also grew an excellent quality of celery.

Paul Bunyan

The best known folk hero of the north woods is the giant lumberjack, Paul Bunyan. He is a product of the logging camps of Michigan, Wisconsin, and Minnesota and his tall tales are full of humor, wit, and exaggeration. According to the stories, it took five giant storks to deliver him to his parents. A lumber wagon and a team of oxen were used as a baby carriage. He would eat 40 bowls of porridge just to whet his appetite. Paul also rescued Babe, his blue ox (as a calf), from drowning during the winter of Blue Snow. Babe grew to be 24 ax handles wide between the eyes and could pull anything that had two ends (except Paul). Paul, it is said, dug Lake Michigan as a drinking hole for Babe.

THE FRUIT BELT

It was during this period that Michigan's fruit belt had its beginnings as a commercial producer of a variety of fruit. Eleven counties along Lake Michigan shore, from the St. Joseph River in the south to the Grand Traverse region in the north—a strip of land about 40 miles wide—were especially productive.

In the extreme southwestern part of the Lower Peninsula is perhaps the most important fruit region in the state. The main fruits grown here are apples, peaches, grapes, and pears. Strawberries, dewberries, raspberries, and blueberries are also grown in large quantities. Muskmelons, tomatoes, and asparagus crops also developed. From Oceana to Grand Traverse counties, cherries and apples are the major fruit crops, while in Oceana peaches are an important crop. Plums and grapes are also grown commercially throughout the region.

Chicago was the nearest and largest market for these crops, but railroads also carried fruit to Detroit and into Indiana and Ohio. The development of canneries and improvements in the preservation process added to the continued success of this industry.

New Mines, New Towns

The Jackson, Cleveland Cliffs, and Lake Superior mines at Negaunee and Ishpeming in the Marquette Iron Range continued to produce iron ore. But after 1870 the type of mining changed. Instead of simple quarrying, it became necessary to sink shafts and run tunnels through solid rock to get at the ore. New tools, such as power drills and hoisting equipment, were necessary and available. New mines opened and new towns sprang up around them. Republic in Manistee County and Champion and Michigamee in Marquette County, all named after the mine or mining company, were some of them. At only 114,000 tons in 1860, production increased to 1,945,000 by 1880. A second railroad built from Negaunee to Escanaba in 1864 gave the mines an outlet on Lake Michigan as well as the one on Lake Superior at Marquette.

In 1877 mines opening on the Menominee Range tapped a new source of iron ore. Iron Mountain, Iron River, and Crystal Falls became the mining centers. Iron Mountain, in Dickinson County, was laid out in 1879 with the opening of the nearby Chapin Mine; Iron River, then in Marquette, now in Iron County, near the Nanaimo Mine was platted in 1881; and Crystal Falls, in the same location and named from the crystal beauty of the falls on the Paint River, was founded in 1880. The Menominee Range had 15 mines by 1880, producing 560,950 tons of iron ore, which was freighted by rail to Escanaba.

Yet a third iron district opened during this period on the Gogebic Range, in the extreme western section of the Upper Peninsula. Rich ore deposits were located in 1881, but development was slow due to the isolation of the region and the lack of transportation in and out of that area. It was the Milwaukee, Lake Shore, and Western Railroad that reached Ironwood in 1884 and made possible the shipment of supplies and ore. The Colby Mine and the Norrie Mine were both producing by 1885, and Ironwood, Bessemer, and Wakefield were the centers of production on this range. The ore traveled by rail to Ashland, Wisconsin, where it was then transferred to ships.

The demands of the Civil War caused the increase in the output of iron ore, and the opening of two additional iron ore regions catapulted Michigan to the leading iron-producing state. By 1890 these three ranges were shipping more than eight million tons of ore yearly to smelters around the Great Lakes.

TRANSPORTATION

The increased production of the Upper Peninsula mines affected the shipping industry of the Great Lakes by inducing the building of newer, larger types of ships. At the beginning the ore was either packed in barrels or simply dumped on the decks of sailing vessels or steamships. In 1869 the "R.J. Hackett" was the first ship designed and built expressly as an iron ore carrier. She was built of wood, steam-powered, and had all her machinery located in her stern and her bridge forward, leaving the space in between for hatches through which the ore could be loaded quickly from the docks at Marquette and Escanaba. Other shipbuilders soon followed suit.

It wasn't long before iron replaced wood, and the first commercial iron ship on the lakes was launched in 1862. Ships made of iron could be built bigger than wooden ones and soon replaced them. The first of the iron bulk freighters, the *Onoko*, was built in 1882 and was 287 feet long.

A rather radical departure from the now familiar bulk freighter made its first appearance in 1888. This boat resembled a submarine, riding low in the water with a rounded topside. It sort of looked like a whale in those days, and it is as a whaleback that it became known. Captain Alexander McDougall, the designer and builder, believed that it could not be destroyed by wind or water. Although no one else thought them unsinkable, their design gave them a certain buoyancy, and whalebacks became quite a common sight on the lakes. They were soon supplanted by the huge bulk freighters, which were more economical to operate.

The great demand for Lake Superior iron ore and the increasing size of the ships made the Sault Ste. Marie locks inadequate. Newer and larger locks were necessary and now, because the work was considered of national importance, the United States government stepped in and began building the Weitzel Lock in 1877. In 1881 Michigan gave the Soo Canal to the United States. The Weitzel Lock opened that same year and was 515 feet long and 80 feet wide. It raised and lowered ships in one step instead of two

The 1885 Eaton County Courthouse, a museum and historic site in Charlotte. Tom Dutcher

as before and charged no toll. In 1887 the Poe Lock was begun and opened in 1896. It was 800 feet long and 100 feet wide. The old state locks were destroyed to make room.

Railroad building greatly increased during this period to keep pace with burgeoning industry. In the Upper Peninsula the railroads transported iron ore, and in the Lower Peninsula they reached the developing lumber centers. By 1872 the Chicago and Northwestern Railroad provided a direct route from Marquette to Chicago.

Michigan capitalists built the Detroit, Mackinac, and Marquette Railroad in order to connect the two peninsulas by rail. It reached from St. Ignace to Marquette in 1881, and ferries crossed the straits to carry railroad cars to the Jackson, Lansing, and Saginaw Railroad Terminal at Mackinac City.

In the Lower Peninsula, a number of new railroads were constructed. Among them were the Flint and Pere Marquette, running from Saginaw to Ludington; the Grand Rapids and Indiana, running from Fort Wayne, Indiana, to Petoskey; the Chicago and Western Michigan, running from

Cherry Festival

The National Cherry Festival is held in Traverse City every year in August. The first commercial tart cherry orchards were planted in 1893 on Ridgewood Farms, near the sight of the original plantings made by Peter Dougherty in 1852. By the early 1900s, the tart cherry industry was established in Michigan from Benton Harbor to Elk Rapids. Michigan is the world's largest producer of tart cherries, and this year's estimated crop of 225 million pounds represents 77 percent of the national crop. The sweet cherry crop is forecast at 60 million pounds, ranking Michigan third behind Washington and Oregon in US production.

New Buffalo in Berrien County to Pentwater in Oceana; and the Toledo, Ann Arbor, and North Michigan Railroad, running from Ohio to Frankfort in Benzie County. The railroad began ferry service from Frankfort to Kewaunee, Wisconsin, in 1892. The TAA&NM was the first to carry freight cars across a body of water as large as Lake Michigan, cutting the time and expense of loading and unloading from car to ship and back again.

At Detroit the rails were quickly connecting the rapidly growing communities of southeastern Michigan. Beginning in 1866, a railroad ferry carried freight and passenger cars across the river to connect the Canadian Great Western and the Michigan Central Railroads. There was talk of building a bridge or a tunnel to speed up the crossing. When ship owners opposed a bridge, lawyer and businessman James F. Joy obtained permission to dig a tunnel in 1871. After several missteps, it was finally completed in 1909.

LEISURE AND LABOR

The demands of the Civil War resulted in an accumulation of wealth in the pockets of more people in Michigan than ever before. The development of the industries in the state created a large group of wealthy individuals and outright millionaires, and they began to spend a portion of this wealth on summer homes and resorts. As early as 1875, the Grosse Pointe area just north of Detroit began to develop into a popular summer resort. The sandy shores of Lake St. Clair were lined with cottages, boathouses, and docks. Some of the cottages were built on a grand scale. The proximity to the lakes led to sailing and rowing regattas as popular sports.

Mackinac Island had been visited by tourists even before the fur trade closed. During the 1850s, some cottages rose up and summer residents found the climate agreeable. After the Civil War, the island became even more popular as a resort. Some hotels arrived and roads grew to connect various points of interest. In 1887 the Grand Hotel was erected by a consortium of steamship and railroad interests, dragging construction materials across frozen water by horse and mule. Built high on a hill, it catered to only the wealthiest of visitors. In 1894 the garrison at Fort Mackinac was permanently removed and the fort was given to the state. The following year almost the whole island was made a state park.

Steamship and railroad companies published illustrated booklets extolling the natural beauty, numerous lakes, and excellent fishing around the state, especially the northern part. The development of resort towns and tourism was largely due

Entrance to Fort Mackinac, located on Mackinac Island
Travel Michigan

to these companies. In addition to Mackinac Island, Petoskey, Charlevoix, and Sault Ste Marie became destination spots.

The Ottawa originally settled Petoskey in Emmet County in the 1700s when hunting and fishing were abundant. The logging industry moved in during the 1850s, but the place only really changed with the arrival of the railroad in 1873. Residents from southern Great Lakes cities such as Chicago and Detroit migrated there, converting the industrial squalor into a town filled with shops and 13 grand hotel resorts by the turn of the century.

Situated between Grand Traverse Bay and Little Traverse Bay, Charlevoix was practically destined to become a vacation destination. Named after French missionary Pierre Francois-Xavier de Charlevoix, resort associations began to plan and settle the site in 1879. Next to Lake Charlevoix, it became a colony for fishermen, its idyllic setting the boyhood stomping grounds of Ernest Hemingway, whose family spent their summers on nearby Walloon Lake.

Charges in these resorts were fairly moderate for the time period. The most expensive advertised rate for room and board on Mackinac Island or at Petoskey was three dollars a day or 18 dollars a week. Room and board could also be had for as little as six dollars a week, with all the hunting, fishing, and sightseeing a person wanted for no cost.

The railroad brochures also emphasized the opportunities for hunting and fishing in Michigan. Fish and game were abundant and there was no limit to the amount of wild turkey, geese, duck, quail, pigeon, deer, and fish any sportsman could take. As early as 1859, the legislature took steps to pass laws to conserve these resources by establishing closed seasons, but the means of enforcement were lacking.

The Fish Commission was appointed in 1873 and focused primarily on building hatcheries to provide a continuing source of lake trout and whitefish. A fish and game warden was appointed in 1887, but even he had little effect on enforcing the laws. Some species soon became scarce and two, the wild turkey and the passenger pigeon, were completely exterminated.

The population of the state of Michigan increased rapidly throughout this period, from 749,113 in 1860 to

Hemingway in Michigan

Ernest Hemingway rarely visited Michigan as an adult, but his childhood summers were spent in and around Walloon Lake, near Petoskey in the northern Lower Peninsula. References to Michigan are constantly popping up throughout his writings, and two of his stories, "Up in Michigan" (taking place in Horton's Bay) and "Big Two-Hearted River" (set in the Upper Peninsula town of Seney), are set in the state. The latter features only one character, Nick Adams. Adams appears in 12 of Hemingway's short stories, including "Ten Indians," whose setting is the area around Petoskey. His fourth book, "The Torrents of Spring," is also set in Petoskey. It involves two main characters, Scripps and Yogi, both of whom work in a pump factory in that city.

2,093,889 in 1890, with the number of foreign-born residents a notable feature. Canadians were the largest element, Germans second, followed by the English, Scots, and Irish. The state legislature actively promoted immigration to Michigan, periodically appointing a commission of immigration and hiring agents to induce people to live in the state. A pamphlet entitled, "Michigan and Its Resources," was widely circulated and translated into different languages. These pamphlets make interesting reading as they listed wages and prices for food and lodging.

New labor unions also sprang up during this period. The Brotherhood of Locomotive Engineers began in Manistee and others among iron molders, blacksmiths, cigar makers, plasterers, and carpenters soon followed. But the Panic of 1873 caused by widespread unemployment considerably weakened the labor movement.

One of the most influential labor organizations in American history rose to power, declined, and disappeared during this period. Like the Freemasons, the Knights of Labor had a lodge, a password, a grip, and secret rituals. It was open to nearly all workers, and a chapter was established in Detroit in 1878. Charles Joseph Antoine Labadie, called

Passenger Pigeons

The passenger pigeon, once the most numerous bird on the planet, made its home in the billion acres of primary forest that once covered the area east of the Rocky Mountains. Their flocks, a mile wide and up to 300 miles long, were so dense that they darkened the sky for hours and days as they passed overhead. Population estimates from the 19th century ranged from one billion to close to four billion birds. The passenger had a slate blue head and rump, slate gray back, and a wine-colored breast. The colors of the male were brighter than the female. Unfortunately, the passenger pigeon was hunted to extinction. The very last bird died in a Cincinnati zoo in 1914.

"the gentle anarchist," was the leader of this branch, which probably numbered between 10,000 and 25,000 members. Knowing that the most good could be accomplished for workingmen by promoting favorable legislation, the Knights entered politics and in 1886 elected 38 members to the state legislature. They were able to help pass laws concerning compulsory school attendance, child labor, required safety devices in factories, and mine inspections.

New laws and safety regulations governing and eventually shortening the work day allowed for more leisure or "off-work" time. People were encouraged to spend more of their day in leisure pursuits. This included bicycling, exercise, and team sports, especially baseball. Beginning in the 1950s, pick up teams and organized amateurs played the national pastime (as it would soon be known) in Michigan on diamonds and sandlots. With the growth of spectator sports, the Detroit Baseball Club organized on a professional level in 1880 and became the newest member of the National League in 1881. Nicknamed the Wolverines, they played their home games at Recreation Park, located at John R. and Brush Streets in Detroit. In 1887 with the addition of Sam Thompson, Dan Brouthers, and Hardy Richardson, the Wolverines claimed the National League pennant and went on to win world championship honors, defeating their American Association rivals in a best-of-fifteen game World

Series. The 1888 season would be their last in the league, as dwindling attendance figures forced their resignation. League officials claimed that Detroit would never be a good baseball town.

NEW BEGINNINGS

As Michigan entered the last decade of the nineteenth century, it found itself at or near the top of the list of the nation's producers in every category, almost as if whatever the people of the state set out to do, they did better than anyone else. For example, former Port Huron resident Thomas Edison invented the practical light bulb, and soon after, Metcalfe's dry goods store in Detroit used them. Grand Rapids resident Melville R. Bissel invented the first carpet sweeper in 1896. In 1879 Detroit telephone customers were the first in the nation to be assigned numbers. And quite by accident, a batch of John Harvey Kellogg's cooked wheat got left out and dried up. Rather than throw it away, he passed it through rollers, creating a whole new eating phenomenon: corn flakes.

All of these accomplishments were just a prelude to what was to come. A new century was just around the corner that would bring with it new ideas, inventions, and unimaginable wealth.

Joseph A. Labadie (1850-1933)

A native of Paw Paw, Labadie roamed the country as a printer and in 1872 put down roots in Detroit working as a printer for the *Detroit Post and Tribune*. He joined the Socialist Party in 1877 and was chosen by the Knights of Labor to organize Detroit's first assembly. By 1883 Labadie had given up socialism for individualist anarchism, and despite his outspoken opposition to government, he was appointed clerk at Michigan's new Bureau of Labor in Lansing. At the age of 50, he began writing verse and publishing artistic hand-crafted booklets. Labadie's extensive collection of labor literature was much sought after by labor scholars, and he decided to donate it to the University of Michigan, where it formed the nucleus of the present-day Labadie Collection.

8

MOTOR CITIES

AGE OF REFORM

The prosperity that had arrived in Michigan by the 1890s also brought with it a certain amount of excess and corruption, and the need for reform was obvious. This problem was nationwide and was not helped by an economic depression known now as the Panic of 1893, occurring shortly after the inauguration of President Grover Cleveland.

The causes for this panic were numerous, but it was precipitated in part by a run on the nation's gold supply—too many people attempted to redeem treasury notes for gold until the statutory limit was reached and no more gold was available. A series of bank failures followed and no less than four major railroads went bankrupt. It was the worst financial crisis thus in the country's history.

This political chaos had its effects in Michigan as the decade ushered in uncertainty in US politics. Not only was Republican rule challenged, but groups demanding greater attention to economic and social questions gathered considerable power. The problem of third parties in Michigan took on slightly different forms in the state. Three distinct groups manifested themselves at this time. The Prohibitionists had a large following among liberal-agrarian factions. A large number of urban voters were unwilling to endorse temperance and subsequently in 1890 formed the Industrial Party. In the same year, an aggressive farm organization, the Patrons of Industry, originating in Port Huron, began to show strength.

All these liberal groups held their conventions almost simultaneously in Lansing, hoping that the three groups would endorse the same candidates, thus fusing into a powerful farmer-labor party. The temperance issue,

Ransom E. Olds (1864–1950)

The first auto factory in Detroit was built in 1900 by Ransom E. Olds, a young wizard from Lansing who had actually built cars before the Duryeas did and just maybe as early as Daimler and Benz in Germany. The first Olds plant was on East Jefferson near the Belle Isle Bridge. He was convinced to build cars in Detroit by one of the lumber barons who financed him. While the plant was being built, Olds and his engineers designed no less than 11 models of different sizes as well as power plants. In March, 1901, a fire destroyed the plant and all but one of the models, a small, light carriage with a curved dash— the model that would put the Oldsmobile on the map.

however, kept the Industrialists and Prohibitionists apart, and the Patrons simply refused all overtures of affiliation. By 1892 the Industrialists and Patrons gave up their separate identities and supported the Populist cause.

The effects of the Panic of 1893 upon Michigan were immediately seen in the closing of several banks. The Central Michigan Savings Bank of Lansing closed its doors on April 18; the First State Bank of Hillsdale, May 10; the Bank of Crystal Falls, June 23; and others later suspended operations. The banks of Detroit, in which many other banks kept deposits, did much to prevent the complete failure of banks and helped stem the panic. Only 15 banks in the state were forced into liquidation by the panic, nine of them being private banks and only one of any size.

The banks were forced to call in their loans when they became due and many businesses, unable to borrow money, were forced to close. The loss of businesses put thousands of men out of work—more than 25,000 in Detroit alone—and overwhelmed Poor Commissions with applications for relief. The effects of this panic disappeared slowly, with business and living conditions not returning to normal for three or four years.

The panic did not adversely affect the fortunes of the Republicans at the polls, as the Democrats were in national

David Dunbar Buick
(1854-1929)

Born in Scotland, Buick emigrated with his parents when he was two years old and as a young man settled in Detroit, where he made a small fortune manufacturing plumbing materials. After seeing his first motorcar around the turn of the century, he became obsessed and in 1902 formed his own auto company, the Buick Manufacturing Company, to make them. His advanced designs left the company constantly in the red, and he had to borrow money from a friend, who convinced him to team up with a company in Flint. He agreed and the new company paid all of David Buick's debts, but the deal left him with little say in the company's activities. After William Durant became general manager, he and Buick were at odds and Buick left. Impoverished, he died of cancer in 1929, though the company and its product still carried his name.

office and hence responsible for the depression. In 1894, the Republicans were victorious, even though the Populists polled over 30,000 votes in the state election. A Republican would sit in the governor's chair until 1913.

HAZEN PINGREE

Of those Republican governors, one in particular distinguished himself, even though his party leadership thoroughly hated him. Hazen S. Pingree, a native of Maine, came to Detroit in 1865, after serving in the Union army. He became a successful businessman as the senior partner in a shoe manufacturing company, Pingree and Smith. By 1890 their business topped the one million dollar mark in sales and Pingree became accustomed to giving and getting his money's worth. In 1889 he was induced to run for mayor of Detroit, a Republican running a city controlled by Democrats, and was reelected three times after that.

Mayor Pingree began immediately to examine the affairs of the city and found that it was being badly cheated out of tax dollars, goods, and services. The electric and gas

companies were overcharging Detroit residents; the street railway company was still using horse-drawn vehicles while charging their customers the going rate of five cents; the few paved streets were full of potholes; and the more affluent city property owners were being assessed at rural rates.

Into this morass of corruption and greed the mayor waded, armed with facts and ready to remedy the abuses. The entrenched interests defied him, something he expected, but many of the best people turned against him, which he didn't. He soon discovered that many of these "friends" were property owners and stockholders in corporations that were robbing the people. They thought that he was one of them, their class. Pingree was snubbed socially, removed from a local bank board, refused business from Detroit banks, but enthusiastically supported by the

Group outside Holmes Motor Company, circa 1930
Willard Library

regular people of Detroit. One of his greatest services as mayor was to awaken those citizens to their duty as voters.

First to be brought to heel was the gas company. Discovering a violation in the terms of its charter, the mayor threatened suit to cancel it. Refusing a $50,000 bribe, Pingree forced company officials to reduce the rate from $1.50 per thousand cubic feet to 80 cents. Unable to do the same to the electric company in 1895, he established a municipal lighting plant, the forerunner of Detroit Edison. Lighting by this plant cost consumers $36 a year per lamp, as opposed to the $140 per lamp as charged in 1889.

Albert Kahn (1869–1942)

An architect of German-Jewish antecedents, Kahn had an extraordinary career as an industrial designer. He is responsible not only for almost all of the major industrial plants of the Big Three and other auto manufacturers in the United States, but also for aviation industry plants, hospitals, banks, commercial buildings, public buildings, temples, libraries, schools, clubs, and over one hundred mansions. In 1904 he applied a new technique, reinforced concrete, to his building designs, allowing for sturdy, spacious, light, and clean factories. After building nine factories for the Packard Motor Company, Kahn decided to use a new method for building number ten. Industrialists were amazed and orders poured in. Kahn built more than 1,000 buildings for Ford and hundreds for GM. He also built office spaces, like the Fisher and General Motors Buildings in Detroit, and private homes, such as the Edsel Ford estate in Grosse Pointe Shores and the Cranbrook House. Some lesser known Kahn masterpieces in Detroit include the Detroit Athletic Club, the Police Headquarters, Liggett School, and the Detroit Golf Club.

Perhaps the incumbent mayor's greatest fight was with the street railways, a conflict that continued through the decade. Pingree found out that the railway companies paid only one and one-half percent of their gross earnings in taxes to the city. In 1890 this amounted to $12,000. He believed they should pay taxes on a fair assessment of their real and personal property as well as reduce the public's fare to three cents. The companies, of course, refused to comply, but in this case they were protected by a 30-year franchise, which would not expire until 1909. Pingree then induced a syndicate to build a three-cent streetcar line in 1895, but this was short-lived. Within less than two years, the line was bought out by the company he was fighting.

When conservative Republicans in the Lansing legislature interfered with his reform plans for Detroit, Hazen Pingree grew convinced that he must be elected governor. In 1896 he obtained the Republican nomination for that office. Despite their fear and abhorration for him, party leaders felt that they needed Pingree's vote-getting power to pull their ticket through—and they were right.

Pingree took office as governor of Michigan in January, 1897, even though his term as mayor of Detroit still had a year to run. For more than two months, he occupied both offices until the state supreme court ruled that he could only be one or the other, not both. He then resigned as mayor and began his state reforms.

AGE OF INVENTION

The changes in technology and methods in manufacturing and other industries fostered an age of invention or, in some cases, an adaptation of known methods to meet new technology. The state of Michigan certainly had its share of both.

The Plymouth Iron Windmill Company began producing their product in 1882 as an aid to farming. Four years later the company was struggling to attract new customers. In 1886 Clarence Hamilton introduced a new idea to the company, a gun that could fire a lead ball using compressed air. Company President Lewis Cass Hough gave it a try and exclaimed, "Boy, that's a daisy!" Very soon after there was a bigger market for their Daisy Air Rifle than their windmills, and with the sale skills of Charles H. Bennett, the company's name was officially changed to the Daisy Manufacturing Company in 1895.

New technologies in construction were plainly seen when in 1890 one of the first skyscrapers in the United States opened at the corner of Fort and Griswold Streets in Detroit. The 10-story Hammond Building was owned by Ellen Barry Hammond, the widow of Indiana meatpacker George H. Hammond. Soon bigger, taller buildings would change the cityscape, such as the Union Trust Building and the Chamber of Commerce Building, both among the first to incorporate a metal skeleton in their construction.

In Detroit a well-known marine engineer named Charles Brady King applied for a patent in 1892 on his invention, a pneumatic hammer. Educated at the University of Michigan, King was fascinated by the new internal combustion engine and went to France to learn all that could be learned about it and its application in a modified carriage.

Two years later, he began secret tests on Belle Isle of his gasoline-powered automobile and, on March 6, 1896, successfully drove his machine, nicknamed "Tootsie," down the streets of Detroit. Assisted by Oliver Barthel, King became the first person in Michigan to accomplish this feat. But more interested in art and music than automobiles, he soon moved on to other things.

Another mechanically minded visionary was more interested and was not too far behind King. Early on the morning of June 4, 1896, 33-year old Henry Ford drove his first gas-powered "quadricycle" through downtown Detroit. Unlike "Tootsie," which broke down on its test drive, Ford was successful and would continue to tinker with his designs over the next three years.

The automotive "fad" wasn't limited to Detroit. Two friends from Lansing, Ransom E. Olds and Frank Clark, whose fathers made gasoline engines and carriages respectively, formed the Olds Motor Vehicle Company in 1897. It was Michigan's first automobile company, and one year later they produced their first car. Like most others of this period, it had only one cylinder—but it ran and would prove to be very popular. Clark sold out to Olds before production could begin and Olds had to find capital investors. Lumber baron Samuel Latta Smith would back Olds financially if he would build his cars in Detroit. Located on East Jefferson Avenue near Belle Isle, the Olds Motor Works opened in 1899 and became the first factory in the country designed specifically to produce automobiles. Machine and tool manufacturer Henry Leland signed a contract to provide transmission gears and other delicate parts for Olds. He had developed processes for tooling machine parts to a fine tolerance of 1/100,000 of an inch and would soon be making a better, more efficient engine for Olds.

The automobile craze was about to turn Detroit and the state of Michigan on its ear. William Metzger opened the first independent dealership at 274 Jefferson Avenue in 1898; the following year, Metzger, along with hardware merchant Seneca Lewis, held the first Detroit Auto Show at the Light Guard Armory, with two electric and two steam vehicles on display. Local capitalists organized the Detroit Automobile Company to produce Ford-designed cars. Entrepreneurs and millionaires, inventors, machinists, and mechanics were about to transform life as it was then known.

The American Century

The last decade of the nineteenth century saw the beginning of the growth of the United States into a world power, and the American Century began with the war against Spain in 1898. The Secretary of War in President McKinley's cabinet was ex-Michigan governor Russell A. Alger. A Civil War veteran who had risen to the rank of major general, Alger returned home to the lumber business and amassed a large fortune. He ran a war department that was woefully inefficient, corrupt, and totally unprepared for war. Although he was a capable administrator, Alger was unable to overcome the deficiencies of the department. Despite the successful conclusion of the conflict, criticisms of the secretary were great, and he resigned to save the president from embarrassment.

Command of the expeditionary force was given to General William R. Shafter, a native of Kalamazoo County. A decorated Civil War veteran, Shafter at this time was 63 years old, ill, and overweight. He managed as well as could be expected, but could barely contend with the illness, tropical heat, spoiled rations, yellow fever, newspaper correspondents, and Theodore Roosevelt.

Monroe Broom Factory, 1901
Monroe County Historical Commission

President McKinley's call for five regiments of volunteers from Michigan was answered with the organization of the 31st, 32nd, 33rd, 34th and 35th infantry regiments. The 33rd and 34th saw active duty in Cuba, the 31st served there after the war on police duty, and the remaining two units never left their southern camps.

Governor Pingree opposed the war with Spain, but when it came he supported the president. He established a camp at Island Lake, near Brighton, and actually lived there with the troops. When they moved to camps at Chickamauga, Georgia, he visited them and did his best to see to their treatment. After the war, he sent special trains to bring the sick and wounded back to Michigan.

Enacted by law in 1893 and finally organized in 1895 was the Michigan Naval Militia. Composed mainly of young men from Ann Arbor, Detroit, and Saginaw, they trained during the summer months on the *USS Yantic*, cruising from Detroit to Mackinac Island. Through an arrangement with Assistant Secretary of the Navy Roosevelt, they were called into active service and sent to Norfolk, Virginia, where they were assigned to a converted merchantman, the *USS Yosemite*, rated as an auxiliary cruiser.

Serving under a regular navy captain, many of the young men came from the leading families of Detroit. Among the crew were John and Truman Newberry, Edwin Denby, Charles B. King, and Henry B. Joy. Denby and Newberry would later serve as secretaries of the navy and Joy would be one of the founders of the Packard Motor Car Company.

The *Yosemite* was first engaged on convoy duty along the east coast and assisted in the US Marine Corps landing at Guantanamo Bay, Cuba. Then she was dispatched to Puerto Rico and successfully blockaded San Juan harbor, destroying a Spanish blockade runner in the process.

PUTTING THE WORLD ON WHEELS

The earlier popularity of the bicycle stimulated, in part, the development of the automobile. During the 1890s the bicycle was transformed from a dangerous high-wheeled vehicle into a safe, chain-driven form of transportation used by a growing number of men, younger women, and older children. The increased use placed an emphasis on greater speed, better roads, and racing. For city dwellers who could not afford to maintain a horse, the bicycle had a particular appeal. It did, however, have its drawbacks. It only accommodated one person and had no protection from the weather. It did not handle rough or muddy roads and was propelled only by leg power. The effort to overcome these limitations led advocates of the automobile to develop a practical horseless buggy.

There were definite circumstances that explain why this new industry developed in Detroit, Flint, Lansing, and other cities in Michigan and not some other state. The financial capital was available; in 1900 there were 44 millionaires in Detroit alone. There was plenty of skilled and unskilled labor available in the area as well. But most significant, perhaps, was the fact that Michigan cities were the centers of carriage, wagon, bicycle, and marine engine manufacture. The carriage industry in Detroit was the second largest in the United States by 1900. Among the carriage makers were William C. Durant, Charles Nash, and the Fisher brothers; bicycle makers included Barney Oldfield and the Dodge brothers, John and Horace; and for 30 years workers had been making marine engines and machine shops were all over town.

Initially, automobile manufacture was geared toward a luxury vehicle and limited market. Early on, two Michigan men, Ransom E. Olds and Henry Ford, conceived the idea of manufacturing moderately priced cars in large scale production. Olds was first in bringing factory methods of production to the industry. His plant on East Jefferson was one that assembled parts, with very little energy devoted to the manufacture of the required materials. Instead, Olds awarded contracts to a large number of other Detroit companies to provide the parts for his cars. Because of the size of these orders, each of the supply plants was able to concentrate its activities on producing these parts, thereby reducing the cost of the product and, subsequently, the car.

The first Olds car carried a sticker price of $1,250 and not many units sold. Back to the drawing board, Ransom designed the curved-dash Olds, weighing 580 pounds and selling for about $650. In 1900 Olds Motor Works sold 1,400 of these cars and 2,100 of them the following year, until a disastrous fire wiped everything out. Relocating to Lansing, Olds' sales in 1902 reached 2,500 units; in 1903, 3,000; and

Dodge Main

The Dodge Brothers built their factory complex, Dodge Main, on a 58-acre site in rural Hamtramck in 1910 with a test track and a hill climb adjacent to the manufacturing plant. It was a city unto itself with 4,500,000 square feet of space available in 59 buildings and included a hospital, private telephone system, and fire department. In the 1940s, approximately 1,200 cars rolled off the assembly lines each day. Despite its past success, Dodge Main was torn down in 1980.

in 1904, 4,000. The Olds was the first cheap car on the market and a pioneer in the light-weight field. "In My Merry Oldsmobile" hit the top ten charts, and cash dividends the first two years amounted to 105 percent.

In 1902 Henry M. Leland and William E. Metzger organized the Cadillac Automotive Company, named after Detroit's founder, Antoine de la Mothe Cadillac. Bent on producing a first-rate car, Leland used his own precisely crafted one-cylinder engine in a passenger car based on a Henry Ford design. The company enjoyed a near instant success, and the Cadillac name would go on to symbolize top quality in automotive standards.

Meanwhile in Flint, a manufacturer of plumbing fixtures had designed a car and organized a company to build it, but David Buick ran out of money before production could begin. He found more in the Briscoe brothers, but in the process lost control of the venture. The Buick emphasized the endurance of its product and first attracted national attention when David Buick made the trip in 1903 from Detroit to Flint without mishap. In 1905 the Durant-Dort Carriage Company bought all rights. It was the first of a few acquisitions to be made by Billy Durant.

In 1899 two sons of a hardware merchant in Warren, Ohio, produced a car that they named after themselves. A solid model and geared toward the higher end of the market, 160 Packards would be sold before the company moved to Detroit in 1903. Detroit investors in Packard included the

Alger brothers, the Newberry brothers, and Henry Bourne Joy. Almost 200 automobiles were produced in 1904.

Without a doubt, the success of the Oldsmobile encouraged new ventures and stimulated public demand for automobiles. The Olds factory served as a training ground for many men who would later on become important figures in the industry. Among these were Leland, R.D. Chapin, and John D. Maxwell. As automobiles became less of a novelty, the customers began to take them seriously—at least those who could afford them. People with money began to feel that they had to have a car in order to be "in the swim." From 1904 to 1908, the greatest success in the business was achieved by those companies producing the higher-priced and heavier cars.

Ford Has a Better Idea

Henry Ford made two false starts before he was successful in producing automobiles. In 1899 the Detroit Automobile Company was organized with Ford as part owner and chief engineer. In 1901 he withdrew from the company over policy differences and organized the Henry Ford Automobile Company, which failed in 1902.

In 1903 the Ford Motor Company was incorporated with a capitalization of $100,000, not all in cash. The backers were Alexander Y. Malcomson, a coal dealer; one of Ford's employees, James Couzens, in charge of business affairs; John Gray, banker; and Horace Rackham and John Anderson, lawyers. Ford held 25 percent of the common stock, and the Dodge brothers were each assigned shares in exchange for manufacturing engine and other parts for the Ford car.

One of Ford's first business partners was a Canadian immigrant named James Couzens, who moved to Detroit in 1890 and worked as a railroad car checker and a coal company clerk at the Malcolmson Coal Co. In 1903 he decided to go into business with Henry Ford and was involved with the founding of Ford Motor Company, rising to vice president and general manager. When Ford regained sole control in 1919, Couzens became a multi-millionaire, selling his stock back to Ford for $35,000,000.

The wealth gave Couzens a chance to give back to the city some of the largesse he gained from it through public service and outright philanthropy. Couzens served as commissioner of street railways from 1913 to 1915; police commissioner from 1916 to 1918; and mayor of Detroit from 1919 to 1922. In November of 1922, he was appointed as a Republican to the US Senate seat vacated by the resignation of Truman H. Newberry. Elected on his own in 1924, Couzens would serve in the senate until his death in 1936, at the age of 64. Perhaps his greatest bequest to Michigan was his establishment of the Children's Fund of Michigan with a 10 million dollar grant.

During the first 15 months of Ford's operations, 1,708 cars were produced at a profit of $280,000. Ford was convinced that people needed autos for everyday transportation and was determined to design and manufacture a dependable, inexpensive product. Orders for his Model A continued to pour in, and soon the Mack Avenue plant became too cramped to keep up with the demand. In 1904 the company moved into newer, larger quarters at Piquette Avenue and Beaubien.

Detroit's first large automobile plant, which "Motor Ae" magazine praised as one of the "new style of factories" and called part of "a movement toward rational working places," was designed by architect Albert Kahn for the Packard Motor Car Company. Construction began in 1903 on East Grand Boulevard, and two years later Building Number 10 was completed. This part of the Packard complex was the first factory built of reinforced concrete in Detroit. Its advantages were immediately apparent to automakers and launched a building boom in the city. Cheaper and easier than steel construction, reinforced concrete allowed for increased floor space and greater expanses of windows for natural lighting due to its strength and rigidity. It was also fireproof.

Shortly after Building Number 10 was completed, work was finished on the Cadillac plant on Cass Avenue, also built with reinforced concrete. Automobile production in Detroit came to almost 20,000 units, making Detroit the auto manufacturing center of America. More was soon to come.

Henry Ford, continuing to design and redesign his cars on the top floor of the Piquette plant, finally realized his dream of an inexpensive, dependable car. In 1908 the first Model T rolled out of the plant, destined to change the

The Michigan State Police

The Michigan Department of State Police began as a temporary wartime security force to provide domestic security during World War I. On April 19, 1917, Governor Albert Sleeper created the Michigan State Troops Permanent Force (also known as the Michigan State Constabulary). This new force consisted of five troops of mounted, dismounted, and motorized units, totaling about 300 men. In 1919 they were reorganized as a permanent, peacetime Michigan State Police, and today they are modern-day law enforcement professionals. Although not the first state police department in the country, they were the first to utilize a state wide police radio system.

world. Selling for $850, it was available with options in a handful of different colors. Ford sold 10,000 of them that first year; however, only 300 were ever built and it was soon evident that a new facility was needed as well as a faster method of construction. Ford bought a 60-acre tract of land in Highland Park, about 10 miles northwest of downtown Detroit and began to make plans to move once again.

Meanwhile in Flint, William Durant established the General Motors Company with Buick as the basis. He had the idea of stabilizing the industry through a strong combination of companies. Capitalized at $12,500,000, he soon acquired the Olds Motor Works. In 1910 he added the Cadillac and Oakland companies, along with parts and accessory manufacturers. After helping to establish the Chevrolet Motor Car Company in 1915, Durant bought it and moved operations from Detroit to Flint.

In 1909 there were 265 establishments making motor cars and some 500 others manufacturing parts. The success of the companies making the larger cars caused other firms to enter the industry. Some survived for a time, others did not. Edward Murphy began building his Oakland car in 1907, later to be called the Pontiac; in 1908 the Paige-Detroit Motor Car Company organized, as well as the Fisher Body Company and Hupp Motors; the following

Monroe police department, circa 1912
Monroe County Historical Commission

year, department store magnate Joseph L. Hudson, believing that people would prefer closed-body cars to open ones, founded Hudson Motors and built the "Essex," starting a trend.

Nearly every city in Michigan at this time could boast of some contribution to the auto industry. Kalamazoo had the "Roamer," built between 1916 and 1926; Saginaw, the "Marquette," in 1912; Jackson, the "Earl," from 1922 to 1924; Adrian, the "Lion" in 1914; and Marysville, the "Wills-Ste. Claire," built from 1921 to 1926.

In 1910 Ford's new Highland Park plant began producing automobiles—all Model T's. The Albert Kahn-designed building was the largest building under one roof in Michigan and would become the industry's model. The main structure was 75 feet wide and 865 feet long. It consisted mostly of poured concrete and glass, with red brick accents at the corners. The glass roof featured as many vents as the walls had windows, providing workers with fresh air, something few factories could boast. Raw materials were delivered to the top floor and made their way down through chutes, conveyors, and tubes, being turned into finished products on the ground floor. People touring the facility were looking at a technological marvel and the future of their city. The city of Highland Park boasted a population of 425 before Henry Ford moved in. Just one year later that figure would reach over 4,000— most of the new residents being employed by Ford. New residential housing, churches, banks, and businesses soon dotted the landscape.

The Dodge brothers, John and Horace, were stockholders in and major parts suppliers for the Ford Motor Company. In 1914 they decided to put their name on their own vehicle. They built America's first mass-produced auto with an all-steel body in a 20-acre plant they constructed in Hamtramck. Dodge Main would soon grow to be the largest automotive manufacturing complex in the world.

While the Dodges were entering the field, Ford was changing the structure of the industry and of society. While he did not invent the moving assembly line, he did adapt the technique to the manufacturing of automobiles. Determined to increase production and consequently reduce costs, Ford had his Highland Park plant designed with the assembly line in mind, the conveyors, pulleys, belts, and hoists making the inside of the plant look like an industrial jungle. Driven by steam and electricity, the plant produced an horrendous noise, but the production time for one car was cut from 12 1/2 hours to 93 minutes by assembling a chassis while it was in continuous motion. By 1915 the annual output was nearly 200,000 Model T's, the cheapest model selling for $360. Accidents to workers in the workplace rose considerably, and absenteeism hit 10 percent with an annual turnover rate of 380 percent among line workers.

In order to stop this turnover and maintain his production rate, Henry Ford declared that the minimum wage for eight hours work would be $5 per day. This astronomical sum was unheard of at this time and drew the wrath of industrialists and other money men down upon Ford's head. Ignoring the criticism, he went ahead with his plan and caused a massive immigration from across the

country, mostly from the deep south to his Highland Park plant. So many men came seeking employment that fire hoses had to be used to disperse a mob of 10,000 at the employment offices. And Ford wasn't finished yet.

LIFE ON WHEELS

The legislature passed the first comprehensive act regulating the use of automobiles in Michigan in 1905. Owners were required to register their cars with the secretary of state. The secretary also required a driver's license before he would issue a small metal disc stamped with a number to be attached to the vehicle. That same number also had to be painted on the back of the car in figures three inches high. In 1910 the state issued two "number plates." The law of 1905 set the maximum speed limit at 25 mph on the highways and 8 mph in the business districts of towns and cities. Drivers also had to defer to horses in all cases.

Unparalleled progress in highway construction accompanied the motor age across the country, and Michigan

A.C. Baker auto dealer, date unknown
Willard Library

contributed in a significant way. The State Highway
Department was created in 1905, and Horatio Earle became
the first state highway commissioner. The state highway
system was perfected in 1913, and courses in highway
engineering began at the University of Michigan in 1912.

Michigan became an outstanding leader in highway
advancement, especially in the development of concrete
pavements, a standard width for pavements (100 feet or
more for right-of-ways), the scientific study of snowfall and
drift, snow removal, the establishment of roadside parks,
the placing of picnic tables, and beautification of roadsides.

As the new century began, so too did an upstart group
of minor league baseball teams—they began calling
themselves the American League and declared that they
were a major league on par with the National League. The
city of Detroit had an entry in this "outlaw" league, who
had been playing their home games on the west side of the

city at the intersection of Michigan and Trumbull Avenues since 1896. The Detroit Tigers would win and break the hearts of generations of fans for decades to come.

In 1905, an 18-year-old kid from Georgia broke into the lineup. Called up in August, Ty Cobb would prove to be one of the greatest baseball players by the time he retired in 1928. The Tigers became the first "3-peaters" as they won the AL pennant in 1907, 1908, and 1909 and failed to win the World Series each time.

Detroit added two more professional sports franchises before World War II. The Detroit Cougars began play in the National Hockey League in 1926, followed in 1934 by the Detroit Lions in the new National Football League. The hockey team played their home games in Windsor, Ontario, Canada, but by the following season the Olympia was opened at Grand River near Temple. The Lions played their home games at the University of Detroit before sharing space at the corner of Michigan and Trumbull. In 1935 all three teams—the Red Wings, Lions, and Tigers—won their respective championships and made Detroit a "City of Champions."

MICHIGAN IN WORLD WAR I

The outbreak of World War I in August, 1914, took most Americans by surprise. Engrossed in their own pursuits, most believed that the war was none of their business, though they felt sympathy for the Allies, especially Britain, France, and Belgium.

But Germany's program of unrestricted submarine warfare eventually led to the sinking of several American ships and the loss of American lives. On April 6, 1917, congress declared war on the Central Powers and Americans were enthusiastic to do their part to defeat them.

In Michigan, Albert E. Sleeper, a Republican, was elected governor in 1916. Late in March, 1917, when war seemed imminent, he called a conference of state officers to consider what actions to take in the event of hostilities. The War Preparedness Board was established and the legislature voted a war loan of $5 million at the request of the governor. This money was used to organize the Michigan State Troops to replace the National Guard units which were then on the Mexican border and expected to be sent overseas. It was also used to aid the families of men in service, provide assistance to returning veterans, and help farmers produce larger crops of necessary foodstuffs.

In an attempt to provide additional protection from lawless elements and foreign saboteurs if necessary, Michigan organized a state police force. These men were to cooperate with state and local agencies in fighting crime and soon became a permanent law enforcing agency.

The 11th National Guard Division was composed of Michigan and Wisconsin men and had been participating in the hunt for Pancho Villa on the Mexican border since January, 1916. After war was declared, this organization became the 32nd Division, nicknamed the "Red Arrow Division," and was sent to Camp MacArthur at Waco, Texas, for training in September, 1917.

Some of the units embarked for France in January, 1918,

Unidentified soldiers at Camp Custer
Willard Library

The Polar Bears

Five thousand American doughboys found themselves on a long, slow trip from England through the Arctic Ocean, not really knowing where they were headed until they disembarked at the Russian port of Archangel. During the closing weeks of World War I, they were sent to fight the Bolsheviks, as the Communists were then called, as part of the American Expedition to North Russia. Among those troops were the 339th Infantry Regiment, the 1st Battalion of the 319th Engineers, the 337th Ambulance Company, and the 337th Field Hospital of the US Army's 85th Division. All have come to be known as "Detroit's Own" or the "Polar Bears" and did not return from their conflict until 1919. There is a special cemetery plot at Holy Cross Cemetery for them, guarded by a huge, white bear.

and by the middle of March, all were reassembled and ready to fight. The division took over a "quiet" sector of the trench line near Belfort, France, in May. In July the 32nd was moved up to the fighting front and went into action on the Ourcq River, taking part in the Battle of the Aisne and the Aisne-Marne offensive under the command of General William G. Haan.

Almost constantly under fire during their war service, the 32nd also participated in the Oise-Aisne and the Meuse-Argonne offensives. One of the best combat divisions, its officers and men were awarded 134 Distinguished Service Crosses as well as numerous other awards by foreign governments—but not without cost. They suffered 2,898 killed and 10,986 wounded. The 32nd served in the Army of Occupation after the Armistice, and units began arriving back in Michigan in April, 1919.

Another unit made up of Michigan and Wisconsin men was the 85th Division. After training at Camp Custer, the division arrived in France in August, 1918. Units of the 85th were broken up and attached to other divisions and Army Corps. Many Michigan men served with the 42nd, or "Rainbow" Division, which contained a unit from every state in the country.

One of the 85th Division's more famous units was the 339th Infantry Regiment, which was detached and sent along with other units to Archangel, Russia, to participate in the Allied campaign against the Bolsheviks. Known as the "Polar Bears," they fought courageously in a losing campaign and did not return to the states until the autumn of 1919. Altogether, some 5,000 Michigan men were killed or died of disease while 15,000 were wounded in the "war to end all wars."

THE HOME FRONT

Michigan contributed to the war effort with her fields and factories as well. Farmers increased production of foodstuffs with the help of the state's War Board, which made arrangements for the purchase of seed and machinery at cost. The factories also produced machinery for the war. Ford Motor produced submarine chasers at its new plant on the River Rouge; Lincoln Motor and Packard produced aircraft and the Liberty engines to fly them; others produced trucks and artillery shells. Homeowners helped out by tending their victory gardens, allowing more produce to reach the front lines. People everywhere in Michigan over-subscribed to each Liberty Bond Drive held during the conflict.

PROSPERITY BEFORE DEPRESSION

The Roaring '20s was a decade filled with great optimism for the future. Industry prospered and there was plenty of work. It was also a decade of lawlessness brought on mostly by ineffective prohibition laws. Michigan had actually voted for prohibition in a statewide election in 1917, to take effect in May, 1918, a full eight months before the rest of the country. By the early 1920s, enforcement of the law broke down and bootleggers became prosperous, popular, and powerful.

Because of its proximity to Canada, the Detroit area became an important center of this new "industry." Cargoes of liquor moved across the Detroit River in every conveyance imaginable practically year-round. In their "Prohibition Navy," the US Customs Patrol had difficulty patrolling the riverfront from Wyandotte to St. Clair Shores.

The Ford Rouge Plant

The largest industrial complex in the world, the Rouge Plant contains 93 structures, 90 miles of railroad tracks, 27 miles of conveyors, 53,000 machine tools, and 75,000 employees. Located on more than 2,000 acres of Dearborn land along the Rouge River just southwest of Detroit, it was built to easily receive iron ore and coal to manufacture its product. Henry Ford developed the Rouge Plant into an almost self-sufficient industrial city. Albert Kahn designed most of the complex, which began producing the new Ford Model A in September, 1927. Through the next 15 years, 15 million cars rolled out of the Rouge. It incorporated all stages of automobile production, from forging steel and stamping to parts manufacture and assembly. Other operations conducted on the site included airplane manufacturing and tractor and shipbuilding. Tours of the Rouge Plant are once again available to anyone interested.

Perhaps due to this problem, Detroit in 1922 became the first city in the nation to use a police broadcasting system and equipped their patrol cars with radios to receive messages.

Also at this time, the last of the "Big Three" automakers made its debut. A former General Motors employee, Walter P. Chrysler, was hired to help save two companies, Maxwell and Chalmers, from financial collapse. In 1925 he organized the Chrysler Corporation and brought out the Plymouth to contend in the low-price field and the De Soto as a middle-price car.

By then, Henry Ford was in the process of transforming Dearborn from a farm district to an industrial one. He had acquired property along the River Rouge, three miles from the Detroit River. Here he was to create the most important factory in all of industrial America. Albert Kahn developed Rouge as a collection of factories, where raw materials entered at one end and finished cars exited at the other. From 1919 to 1926, Rouge grew to include 93 buildings, and 75,000 employees produced 4,000 cars per day. It had the largest steel foundry in the world, and its electric power plant could have serviced a city of 350,000 people, making the Highland Park plant obsolete.

This prosperity was not to last, however. Economic conditions across the country would soon change, culminating in the stock market crash of October, 1929. The great depression of the 1930s would hit Michigan hard as the majority of its economy was industry, especially automotive, based.

During this period, Michigan modernized as automobiles altered life, work, and business forever. The population of the state grew as people migrated north in search of better jobs. There was a great shift in population from the rural to the urban areas, and Michigan cities grew tremendously. The make-up of that population changed as well, with more people of eastern European ethnicity arriving everyday, along with a great influx of African Americans in numbers never before imagined.

9

THE GREAT DEPRESSION AND THE ARSENAL OF DEMOCRACY

THE LIVING PAST

On September 27, 1928, in a well attended, well publicized event, Henry Ford cut the ribbon on his monument to the past, Greenfield Village. Although well known for his comment, "History is bunk!", Ford built this monument in recognition of the achievements of man in his working world. A collection of original buildings from across the country (starting with Thomas Edison's laboratory from New Jersey), it was modeled on the Rockefeller Foundation's Colonial Williamsburg in Virginia. One year later, on October 21, 1929, the Henry Ford Museum was dedicated while celebrating the golden anniversary of the invention of the electric light bulb. Thomas Edison and President Herbert Hoover were among the honored guests.

In addition to this tribute to man's genius, other marvels were also in evidence. Across Oakwood Boulevard was the Albert Kahn-designed Dearborn Inn, the world's first airport hotel, servicing passengers and pilots using the Ford airport, dedicated in January, 1925. The Ford Motor Company had crossed into the commercial aviation field with the acquisition of the Stout Airplane Company and designer William Stout. The Ford Tri-Motor was one of the first passenger carriers and one of the safest aircraft in the skies.

Another monument to progress was the Ambassador Bridge, opened to traffic on November 15, 1929. Its 9,602 feet spanned the Detroit River from Detroit to Windsor, Ontario, and is the longest international bridge in the world. Not satisfied with driving over the river, a vehicular tunnel under the riverbed was completed and opened to traffic just one year later. At 5,135 feet in length, the

The Dearborn Inn

The Dearborn Inn is a 222-room historic hotel built in 1931 to accommodate overnight travelers arriving at the Ford Airport, which was located just across the street on Oakman Boulevard. Designed by Albert Kahn, it was the world's first airport hotel. The Georgian-style structure features a crystal-chandeliered ballroom and high ceilings. The guest quarters along Pilots Row were originally used by the airlines' crews. In 1937 accommodations were expanded with the addition of replicas of historic houses and included the Patrick Henry House, the Edgar Allan Poe House, and the Walt Whitman House.

Detroit-Windsor Auto Tunnel provides access to Canada from the downtown area.

Building in Detroit proceeded at a rapid pace during the 1920s, with public buildings, hotels, movie palaces, and skyscrapers transforming the skyline and ranking the city third nationally in new construction. Examples include the Women's Hospital, the 13-story David Stott Building, the Union Produce Terminal, the Fox Theater, the Vanity Ballroom, and the Scarab Club Building.

The rich and powerful were also busy constructing their mansions in and around the city. Edsel and Eleanor Ford moved into their new home on Lake Shore Drive in Grosse Pointe Shores, fully equipped with swimming pool, lagoon, boathouse, and a 3/4 scale dollhouse. Construction was completed on Alfred and Matilda Wilson's home in Oakland County and named Meadowbrook Hall. While over in Bloomfield Hills, the Cranbrook School opened for business. The Booths, George and Ellen, purchased a large farm in 1904 and added several buildings, including an art academy, to the property since then.

This building boom soon came to a screeching halt in late October, 1929, with the stock market crash that ushered in the great depression.

The Great Depression

Just as tourism became one of the leading sources of income in Michigan, the stock market crash of October, 1929, and the economic depression that followed put a temporary halt to just about everything of a progressive nature. One of the many building projects cancelled was a proposed 70-story second Book Tower along Washington Boulevard in Detroit.

The catastrophe hit the automobile industry as production fell from more than 5,000,000 units in 1929 to a low of 1,300,000 units in 1932. The number of manufacturers fell until by the end of the decade only seven—the Big Three of Ford, GM, and Chrysler and four smaller companies—were still in business. As Michigan was intimately tied to the auto industry, this drop in production and subsequent loss of jobs had a devastating effect on the state. Thousands abandoned the fruitless search for jobs, leaving the cities for the less stressful, less expensive life in the countryside. By 1934 nearly one in six Michigan citizens depended upon some form of relief. Farmers suffered severe losses as well and the Upper Peninsula's mining industry almost collapsed completely.

But a new interest in politics also characterized the decade, along with an emphasis on economic reform greater than had been known previously. Both political parties were dedicated to policies of change, although the Democratic platform was the more radical of the two. Suddenly, Michigan became a politically doubtful state. For the first time since 1852, the people of Michigan voted for a non-Republican president when they helped elect Franklin D. Roosevelt in 1932. They even elected a Democrat for governor, William A. Comstock.

One of President Roosevelt's most vigorous supporters was a Roman Catholic priest from Royal Oak. The Reverend Charles A. Coughlin was the pastor of the Shrine of the Little Flower and had a radio program/pulpit from which he espoused on everything and anything political, economic, and religious. Advocating reforms and attacking Communism and later Jews, Coughlin gained a wide following. He vehemently attacked President Hoover, bankers, and industrialists who were, he claimed, to blame for the condition which existed. He advised his listeners that the alternatives were Roosevelt or ruin.

In Detroit, thousands were out of work with no money to buy the necessities of life. Fortunately, a man named Frank Murphy was in the mayor's seat. A World War I veteran and former judge of the Recorder's Court, Murphy was determined that no one should starve, so he spent money on food for the hungry and opened an abandoned warehouse as a barracks for homeless men. He also permitted outdoor mass meetings, held in Grand Circus Park, for those wishing to criticize the political and economic system as was their right. Elected to succeed the recalled Charles Bowles, Murphy was sharply criticized by many citizens who felt he was wasting money on idlers and encouraging the spread of Communism by permitting radicals to talk. In 1933 President Roosevelt appointed him to the post of governor-general of the Philippines. Frank Murphy would return in 1936, just in time to be elected as Michigan's governor.

As the "Radio Priest" turned his attacks against the president he once supported, the most furious events of Michigan's Depression era began. It was in the automobile plants where the struggle for unionization exploded into violence. Unionism had hardly made an inroad into the industry before the 1930s. The American Federation of Labor had organized some of the skilled tradesmen but refused to deal with the large pool of unskilled line workers, because they did not fit into any particular craft. The auto manufacturers were convinced that the open shop concept was crucial to their success, leaving the workers without any protection whatsoever. They could be laid off or fired for any reason, including giving a foreman the evil eye. The monotonous and exhausting work was made worse by the "speed up," an increase in the tempo of the assembly line. As the Depression continued, the work was more irregular and the average weekly pay fell.

Automobile workers grew increasingly restive as the Depression worsened. Three thousand unemployed marched on Ford's Rouge plant in March, 1932, demanding jobs, only to be met with tear gas and gunfire from the Dearborn police. Four men were killed and 24 wounded, setting off spontaneous and unsuccessful strikes in several Detroit auto factories throughout the year.

In August, 1935, the American Federation of Labor

The Flint Sit-Down Strike

On December 30, 1936, several thousand UAW members at three General Motors factories in Flint began a strike against their employer. What they wanted was simple: GM recognition of the union. For over six weeks the strikers stopped production and refused to leave the plants, sleeping on unfinished car seats and eating food their families and friends slipped them through the windows. Less than 44 days later, they emerged victorious. Calling for supporters to gather at Cadillac Square in Detroit, 150,000 people responded in a surprising show of strength for the strikers. Other union workers held sympathy strikes, closing plants in other states. In all, 17 GM plants were shut down. After several battles with police and intervention by the governor and President Franklin Roosevelt, GM and the UAW reached an agreement. Among the issues won by the union were a 5 percent pay hike, recognition of the UAW as the sole bargaining group, seniority rights, overtime pay, and the right to speak in the lunchroom.

(AFL) called a convention in order to consolidate its various automotive locals into the United Automobile Workers (UAW) union, with paid-up membership amounting to only 22,687 workers, 3,610 of whom were from Michigan. Before the year was out, the UAW left the AFL, absorbed several competing unions, and affiliated itself with the Congress of Industrial Organizations (CIO), headed by John L. Lewis and others and founded to organize the mass production industries.

With the assistance of Lewis and the intervention of Governor Frank Murphy, the UAW established its presence in the auto industry by winning a monumental six-week strike against General Motors, beginning in late December, 1936. In a bold change of strategy, UAW officials seized installations in Flint and held a sit-down strike instead of picketing from the outside. Governor Murphy rushed National Guard troops in to preserve order, while UAW forces beat back attacks by Flint city police. The company and union reached an agreement on February 11, 1937, with GM consenting to enter into collective bargaining with the

The Battle of the Overpass

After a series of successful strikes against several of Detroit's auto manufacturers and parts producers, UAW leaders felt the time was right to go after the Ford Motor Company, the hardest case of them all. Henry Ford had said that he would never cave to the unions, that he didn't like their politics or the control they had over companies and workers. The UAW developed a leaflet campaign and made plans to hand them out at the Ford Rouge Plant Miller Road overpass at Gate 4. It obtained permits from the city of Dearborn, and on May 26, 1937, Walter Reuther and his associates were there to hand the leaflets out. About 25 men from Ford's "service department" were also there to prevent them from doing so. The service men attacked the union members, inflicting tremendous injuries to Reuther, Richard Frankensteen, and Robert Kanter, among others. News photographers were there and one of them managed to smuggle out his photos. The ensuing publicity meant bad news for Ford worldwide, and three years later the company signed a union contract.

UAW. Within six months of the Flint victory, UAW membership ballooned to 525,000 members.

Chrysler and other parts manufacturers surrendered to the union shortly after, leaving the Ford Motor Company as the last hold out. Henry Ford was vehemently against the UAW and his chief lieutenant, Harry Bennett, assembled a pug-ugly collection of prize fighters and thugs into the Ford Service Department. Within the Rouge, they were a threatening presence, effectively discouraging organizers. In May, 1937, a group of these Ford Service men brutally beat a delegation of UAW leafleteers on an overpass leading to the main gate at the Rouge plant. Victims of the attack included Walter P. Reuther and Felix Frankensteen, with Reuther soon to emerge as a UAW leader.

ROAD TO RECOVERY

By the middle of the 1930s, some degree of recovery from the effects of the Depression become visible in the Detroit area. The employment rate was above the national level and the number of income tax returns in 1940 for Michigan was 145.2 per 10,000 people. Throughout the United States that figure was only 111.7.

The development of new sources of wealth contributed to this recovery. First among these was the petroleum industry, which brought wealth to many sections of the state. The demand for petroleum products, resulting from the growth of the automotive and aviation industries, led to a renewed search for oil in Michigan. Monroe County produced a small amount of petroleum, and larger fields developed in the Saginaw and Muskegon areas. By 1939, 479 wells were drilled in 46 of Michigan's 83 counties. The state owned a considerable amount of the oil-bearing land, having acquired the titles to this land because of tax delinquencies. In 1938 the state government received over $500,000 from oil royalties, bonuses, and rentals.

The tourists trade also became a large scale industry during the thirties. The widespread improvement of highways made it possible for large numbers of people to reach the northern portions of the state with relative ease, and lakes and towns not located on main highways became attractive resort centers. The weekend tourist became as important to resort towns as the seasonal guest. The recreational possibilities of Michigan were not limited to the summer months either. Snow trains ran on weekends from Detroit to Grayling for skiers and other winter sports enthusiasts. Tourist associations representing various areas across the state advertised the attractions and advantages of both Peninsulas. Manistee, Traverse City, Charlevoix, Petoskey, Mackinac City, Alpena, Grayling, and Marquette are among the many cities that are now resort destinations.

The beginning of national defense activities in 1940 stimulated all phases of Michigan industrial life, accelerated by the outbreak of World War II. The state placed third in the value of new plants, conversions, and expansions with over $778,000 worth of new plants constructed to supplement the industries that converted to war production.

ARSENAL OF DEMOCRACY

During the epic struggle that was World War II, Detroit became known as "The Arsenal of Democracy." The entire state earned that sobriquet as the $29 billion worth of war munitions produced by Michigan industries across the state surpassed all other states. The list is impressive and includes four million engines, 2.6 million trucks, nearly 50,000 tanks, 27,000 complete aircraft, 245 million shells, and nearly six million guns. This output represented fully 70 percent of Michigan's production and 35 percent of the nation's.

Leading this dynamic city was its mayor, Edward J. Jeffries, Jr., a native Detroiter and son of a veteran Recorder's Court judge. Winning a seat on Detroit's Common Council in 1932 and its presidency in 1838/39, the younger Jeffries defeated a corrupt incumbent, Richard Reading, in 1939 to begin a four-term tenure as mayor. Jeffries was committed to public citizenship and had a reverence for Detroit as the center of active life. He felt it his duty to enhance the quality of life for the socially and economically disadvantaged and strove to make the city a single but diversified body united in the common goal of a good city. He was a bright, articulate man who bowled as well as golfed and would see Detroit through some very tense days in the years to follow.

The plants that some of these products came out of were nothing short of spectacular. In April, 1941, construction began on what would be the largest assembly plant built up to that time, the Willow Run bomber plant near Ypsilanti. Hailed as one of the seven wonders of the world, Henry Ford proposed to mass produce one B-24 Liberator heavy bomber every 60 minutes. Although the first one wasn't finished until September, 1942, 42,000 workers produced over 8,600 bombers by war's end.

In August, 1940, ground was broken on the $20 million Albert Kahn-designed Chrysler Tank Plant in Warren, Michigan. A mere six months later, the first tank rolled off the assembly line. The Detroit Tank Arsenal and the General Motors Tank Arsenal near Flint would produce nearly 50,000 tanks for the war.

Unlike World War I, manufacturing was not confined to the larger cities during World War II. Ludington, with a new $22 million chemical plant, rated 13th among 26 manufacturing areas placed in war production. Naval vessels were produced in a number of places, including some inland cities. Cadillac, for example, produced a number of landing

A monarch pine at Hartwick Pines State Park near Grayling
Travel Michigan

Willow Run and the Arsenal of Democracy

In April of 1941, ground was broken for the construction of an airplane factory, the size of which the world had never seen. Designed by Albert Kahn, the factory had 3.5 million square feet of factory space, prompting Charles Lindberg to call it "the Grand Canyon of the mechanized world." Soon a veritable city grew up around the plant to accommodate the expected 100,000 workers, a highway was built, and the Michigan Central Railroad ran trains to ease the commute from Detroit to Willow Run. After the bombing of Pearl Harbor and the country's entry into World War II, production began in earnest and by the war's end the plant built almost 9,000 B-24 bombers.

craft, while shipyards in Bay City and Marquette built sub chasers, destroyer escorts, and towing craft, respectively.

The Dow Chemical Company processed magnesium at Ludington and Marysville and created dozens of chemically-based war products at its main plant in Midland. One of these products, a plastic package wrap called "Saran," was thought to have postwar commercial possibilities. The Kellogg Company of Battle Creek produced millions of units of its wartime specialty, the "K" ration. A factory in Petoskey turned milkweed pods collected by Michigan school children into filler for life jackets instead of kapok, an item cut off from use by the Japanese. A company in Monroe made clay pigeons for target practice; a firm in Grand Haven built soda fountain equipment for the army's post exchanges; and inmates at the Jackson and Ionia state prisons produced cotton shirts and twine.

Michigan's greatest contribution to the war effort consists of over 600,000 men and women who served in the armed forces between September 1940 and December 1945. Over 14,000 of these were among the missing and dead in the conflict. They served in all branches of the armed forces, including the Coast Guard and the Nurse Corps, in all theaters of the war. Michigan's National Guard had been

Detroit Arsenal Tank Plant

This tank arsenal was the first ever built for the mass production of American tanks. Springing up almost overnight in the winter of 1941/42, it was owned and operated by Chrysler. It received its first contract for 1,000 M3 tanks in 1940 and presented the first vehicle in April, 1941, before the plant was completed. The plant also built the M4 Sherman tanks and set an all-time monthly production record by delivering 896 M4's in December, 1942. The Detroit Tank Arsenal Plant built a quarter of the 89,568 tanks produced in the United States overall.

called into federal service in October 1940 and served with Wisconsin men in the 32nd Division, known as the "Red Arrow" for its swift movements through France and Germany during World War I.

Elements of this division were trained at Fort Sheridan, Illinois, and Fort Knox, Kentucky, and were scheduled to fight in the Southwest Pacific. The division embarked on transports at San Francisco, California, in April, 1942, and landed in South Australia. They then moved to Brisbane on the east coast with New Guinea, north of Australia, as their battle target. Beginning in September, 1942, they made contact with the Japanese on the island, fighting their way through rancid jungles and the rugged terrain of the Owen Stanley Mountains until April, 1943, when the 32nd returned to Australia for a rest. They had to return to New Guinea that September to finish up and added Leyte and Luzon to their battle honors. They were still in action in the Philippines when V-J Day was proclaimed.

THE HOME FRONT

While Michiganders were fighting overseas, others received their training and education in the state. Several large training camps were established and others, such as Fort Custer, near Monroe, and Selfridge Field, near Mt. Clemens, were reutilized. The naval base on Grosse Isle trained hundreds of naval aviators, while Coast Guard

Scene at Camp Custer
Willard Library

stations in Port Huron and other cities along the lake shore trained thousands of seamen.

Higher education was absolutely necessary for carrying on the war and Michigan's colleges and universities participated in the war-training programs. All of them accelerated their schedules and held continuous classes throughout the year. Michigan State College had army specialized training groups in engineering, area, and language, while the University of Michigan had the Judge Advocate General's School and the Army Japanese Language School, among others.

With the men off to war, the women gladly took their places building tanks, trucks, and bombers. Rosie the Riveter became part of a government-sponsored adver-

tising campaign that recognized the contributions women made during the war. At least half of these women had never worked out of the home before, and of the estimated 200,000 women working in the auto plants, 75 percent of them wanted to remain on the job. The rest returned to the home when the veterans came back.

10

A Changing State

Return to Normalcy

As the war ended, Michigan looked forward to a return to normal. The efforts to shake off the effects of the Great Depression were starting to show signs of success by the end of the 1930s, but were then interrupted by the devastating events of the war in the first half of the 1940s. The automobile industry in particular was looking forward to reconverting back to making and selling new cars. In 1945 over 25 million cars were still on the road, even though no new cars had been produced since 1942. A great many of these were ready for the junkyard, and with Americans now ready to spend the money they couldn't because of rationing, Detroit was preparing for a postwar boom.

Advanced planning helped to speed up the reconversion of war plants to civilian production. After the surrender of Germany in May, 1945, war production decreased, and during the summer plants made some progress toward retooling. When Japan surrendered that August, war contracts were cancelled and reconversion began in earnest. By the end of 1945, 75,000 cars had been built, albeit refurbished versions of 1942 models, enough to supply two cars for each of the 33,000 dealerships across the country. This scarcity created a seller's market, something that had not been the case since the beginning of the auto industry, and for several years any car that was produced immediately sold.

This phenomenon allowed smaller, independent auto companies to enter the market and enjoy good sales. Preston Tucker, a native of Ypsilanti, made a splash with his Tucker Torpedo until he was forced out of business in 1949. A more serious new entry in the car business was made by Henry J. Kaiser, a California businessman who partnered up with Detroit auto magnate Joseph W. Frazer

The Automobile Hall of Fame

Opened in August, 1997, the Hall of Fame is adjacent to the Henry Ford Museum and Greenfield Village in Dearborn. It tells the story of the automobile through the people whose vision brought the industry to life. Benz, Ford, Olds, and others are all represented here and the result is a brand new experience for the visitor. There is over 8,000 square feet of permanent exhibits. Organized in 1939 to perpetuate the memories of industry giants and innovators, the hall resided in New York City, Washington, DC (1960), and Midland, Michigan (1971), before moving to Dearborn. Over 200 individuals have been inducted and nearly 30,000 visitors are welcomed each year.

to build automobiles. An expert in the mass-production of ships during the war, Kaiser obtained the government-owned Willow Run bomber plant, which the Ford Motor Company decided not to keep. By 1946 low-priced Kaisers and high-priced Frazers came off the line, and in two years they accounted for 5 percent of all new car sales in the country, an impressive feat not seen since the rise of the Big Three in the twenties. By 1950, however, the company was all but finished and in 1955 was producing only the Jeep.

By 1949 auto production finally surpassed the record year of 1929, and the seller's market came to an end, putting the smaller companies out of business. No one could compete with the Big Three's superior manufacturing facilities and extensive network of experienced dealers. Americans wanted bigger, better cars, and Ford, Chrysler, and General Motors were ready give them what they wanted. In 1949 GM designer Harley Earl stuck tail fins on the Cadillac and an era began that lasted over a decade.

As Michigan's automobile industry gained supremacy, so too did the worker's union, the UAW. During the war, a moratorium on strikes had mostly been honored, and when peace arrived the relationship between labor and management was near what it had been during the 1930s. The test of strength came in November, 1945, when the UAW struck GM. Led by Walter Reuther, the strike was successfully settled in March, 1946, the workers gaining some fringe benefits and a 15 percent wage increase. That same month, Reuther was elected president of the union by a narrow margin and gained control of the executive board the following year. He would remain in control until his death in 1970, using the union's power to influence the development of social programs and other humanitarian reforms.

THE FABULOUS '50S

The 1950s were notable for more remarkable changes than any similar period in history. In the Western world and the United States in particular, economic conditions improved immensely. Americans had more of everything—houses, televisions, cars, money, leisure time, and more—and perhaps nowhere was that truer than in Michigan. The economic prosperity of the decade brought about many changes and improvements in the state.

The celebration of Detroit's 250th birthday in 1951 saw the construction of many buildings along and near the riverfront. The Veteran's Memorial Building was the first to open in the new Civic Center area in June, 1950, and plans were announced to build the Henry and Clara Ford Memorial Auditorium. The Detroit Historical Museum opened the doors to its new building on Woodward Avenue at Kirby Street. A fundraising campaign also began for a new convention and exhibits building in the Civic Center and a community arts building on Wayne State University's campus. The highlight of the year-long celebration was a grand parade down Woodward Avenue.

Just in time for summer fun, the St. Clair Metropolitan Beach opened on June 23, 1951. Developed by the Huron-Clinton Metropolitan Authority, it remains a vacation destination for Michiganders.

The decade that was the 1950s also saw many more cultural icons come into being. The J.L. Hudson's department store in downtown Detroit was in its heyday, occupying 40 acres of space in its multistory building. The store employed 12,000 people, making as many as 100,000 sales per day. Its five restaurants served 14,000 meals each day, including their signature Maurice salad.

In time to help celebrate its 50th anniversary in 1953, the Ford Motor Company reopened its ultra modern Ford

Rotunda in Dearborn. That same year Chevrolet introduced the Corvette, the first true American sports car. In 1954 Ford introduced the Thunderbird in an attempt to keep up with the competition.

As automobiles were rolling off the assembly lines and into garages, improvement in transportation systems were underway, none greater than the freeway system. Although the state's first freeway, the Davison, was opened in 1942, the 1950s saw a number of systems opened across the state and country. In 1953 the first section of the John C. Lodge freeway opened, followed by the Edsel Ford (I-94), the Walter Reuther (I-96), and the Fisher (I-75). Over 17,000 Detroiters were displaced by these freeways and more than one neighborhood was either divided or obliterated altogether. This forced diaspora helped develop several suburban areas, as city dwellers became suburbanites.

These freeways continued across the state. The five-year road building program, begun in 1957, quintupled the miles of freeway from 101 to 537 by 1960, placing Michigan first in the nation in interstate highway construction. Perhaps the greatest achievement of the construction projects during this time period was the building of the Mackinac Bridge, linking the two peninsulas. Beginning work in 1954, contractors laid the foundations 206 feet below the lake level and raised the main towers to a height of 525 feet above the water. The work was completed in 1957 and the bridge was opened to traffic in November. The total length of the suspension bridge is 8,614 feet, then the longest in the world. With the approaches included, the Mighty Mac is five miles long.

Throughout the war years, professional sports was played at a lower skill level as major league players were drafted or enlisted into the armed forces. The Tigers won a pennant in 1940 and a World Series in 1945—but that was it for all teams. As the '50s began, the Red Wings and Lions were both poised to become perennial winners of their respective championships; some might even have called them dynasties.

The Red Wings won the Stanley Cup in 1950, 1952, 1954, and 1955; the Lions won the NFL title in 1952, 1953, and 1957—the same year the city acquired its fourth professional sports team when the Fort Wayne Pistons moved to Detroit as part of the National Basketball Association.

The R.E. Olds Transportation Museum

Located on Museum Drive in Lansing, Michigan, the Olds Transportation Museum is an outstanding destination for the vintage auto enthusiast as well as the average viewer. Not only can one see the oldest Oldsmobile, but one can also view the fastest and the rarest of the vehicles. The last Oldsmobile rolled off the assembly line in April, 2004, marking the 35,229,218th vehicle built since the first in 1897. The dark red Oldsmobile Alero is the last of 500 commemorative cars to wear the special paint, badging, and medallion. Oldsmobile was responsible for some of the most stylish and innovative additions to automobiles. Chrome Plating was introduced in 1925; automatic transmissions standard in 1940; Rocket V8 power in 1949; the Jetfire turbocharged fuel-injected engine in 1962; front wheel drive in 1966; and air bags in 1974.

The Detroit Tigers would finally break through and win the AL pennant in 1968 after a heartbreaking loss the previous year. After falling behind the St Louis Cardinals three games to one, they rallied behind the pitching of World Series MVP Mickey Lolich to claim their first world championship since 1945.

THE TURBULENT '60S

The population of Michigan increased by 1.5 million souls from 1950 to 1960, a gain greater than any other state in the Old Northwest. Then a decline began and research showed that 200,000 people had migrated to other states between 1957 and 1960. The cause of this exodus was the reduction in the manpower demands of the automobile and related industries. The federal census of 1960 showed that larger cities had lost rather than gained population. Many were moving out of the cities to the fringe areas outside the city limits due to the great increase in births, overcrowded schools, small city lots, insufficient parking spaces, and high taxes.

High wages and easy home financing also enabled the building of subdivisions and these areas gradually grew large enough to become cities of their own. Shopping became more convenient as supermarkets and large centers were established. The first in the nation was the Northland Center, which opened in Southfield in 1954, boasting more than 50 stores and parking for more than 10,000 cars. Followed by Eastland Mall in 1957, they served as models for shopping centers around the country.

New cities that developed from fringe settlements included Southfield, incorporated as a city in 1958; Livonia, 1950; Oak Park, 1945; and Wayne, 1960. Older cities, such as Saginaw, Jackson, Pontiac, and Monroe, continued to lose population, while Flint and Grand Rapids added very little. These losses resulted in a reduction in revenue from the state and forced cities to implement new taxes to make up the loss.

Fall view of the Au Sable River near Oscoda
Vito Palmisano

Population losses not withstanding, Michigan entered the decade developing some small, new industries that would become synonymous with the state. In 1959 Mike Ilitch opened Little Caesar's Pizza Treat in Garden City, followed one year later by Tom Monaghan's Domino's Pizza Outlet in Ypsilanti. Former automaker Berry Gordy, Jr., bought a house on West Grand Boulevard in Detroit and put up a sign reading "Hitsville, USA." And in 1961 Motown had its first number-one hit, "Please Mr. Postman" by the Marvelettes. All three of these men were to have a profound effect on their state.

The changes that were occurring throughout the country with regards to the economy, the escalating war in

Harley Earl (1893–1969)

Harley Earl did for car design what Henry Ford did for the automobile. Born in California to well established parents, he left Stanford University to study auto design at his father's company, the Earl Automotive Works. They did custom design work for Hollywood's top stars and movie company owners and had as customers Cecil B. De Mille, Tom Mix, and Fatty Arbuckle, among others. Earl Automotive was sold to General Motors and Earl went to work for them in 1927. When he retired from GM, he left behind him designs using classic chrome, two-tone paint, tail fins, hardtops, and wrap-around windshields.

Vietnam, and race relations were to have a dramatic effect on the people of Michigan. The recession of the late 1950s and early 1960s affected the automobile industry, and the resulting loss of jobs added to the burden of many Michiganders, especially African Americans.

The African-American population of the state continued to increase at a constant pace. The 1960 census revealed a non-white population of nearly 800,000, or almost 9.4 percent of the total. In Detroit, about 30 percent of the city's residents were African Americans. African Americans were able to get better jobs, becoming teachers, police officers, and skilled and professional workers; but in spite of an increasing African-American middle class, segregation in housing practices continued and many could not obtain houses outside of the ghettos. The general prosperity of the nation made this poverty even more galling. The economic gap led many to become outspoken critics of the continuing discrimination and part of the new, vigorous civil rights movement.

The most prominent leader of the civil rights movement, Dr. Martin Luther King, Jr., sought to use non-violent means in achieving his goals. On June 23, 1963, Dr. King came to Detroit to lead a non-violent protest. Nearly 125,000 people participated in the Peace March down Woodward Avenue to Cobo Hall in the riverfront Civic

Center. Leading the march with Dr. King was Walter Reuther, former Michigan Governor John Swainson, Detroit Mayor Jerome P. Cavanaugh, and other whites who wanted to show their support.

Dr. King declared that the march was the largest such demonstration that had been held anywhere in the country. Climaxing the day's event, King gave a speech in Cobo Hall. In that speech, he previewed the famous "I Have a Dream" speech he would give at the Lincoln Memorial in Washington, DC, two months later.

But non-violent protest did not solve the problem of civil rights, and the country exploded into catastrophic riot and chaos. In the summer of 1965, the worst riot since 1943 ravaged the African-American section of Los Angeles, Watts. There was rioting in Chicago the following summer, and on July 23, 1967, Detroit took its turn. One week later, 43 people were dead and thousands injured. Property damages were conservatively set at around $50 million as 2,509 stores were destroyed and hundreds of residences burned. Fourteen other cities in Michigan, including Pontiac, Grand Rapids, Flint, Saginaw, and Kalamazoo, suffered racial disturbances during that long, hot summer. Detroit's reputation as a model city went up in flames, along with the future political career of its accomplished mayor, Jerome P. Cavanagh.

Born, raised, and educated in Detroit, Jerry Cavanagh was one of its most dynamic mayors and helped mold modern Detroit. This 31-year-old stunned the political world by upsetting incumbent mayor Louis Miriani in a storybook campaign reminiscent of John F. Kennedy. The following four years saw a city radically changing with newly instituted and enforced fair employment policies for city hiring; the beginnings of a transformed police department; and over $230 million from the federal government for redevelopment and social services. But all this and the promise of more could not overcome Detroit's history of bad race relations.

With a city on fire around him, Cavanagh himself stated, "Today we stand amidst the ashes of our hopes. We hoped against hope that what we had been doing was enough to prevent a riot. It was not enough."

The response to the tragedy was two-fold. The Michigan legislature listened to popular demand for tighter law

The Mackinac Bridge

The Mighty Mac is one of the world's most beautiful bridges and the longest suspension bridge in the Americas with a total length of 8,614 feet suspended. It is currently the third longest suspension bridge in the world. Ground was broken to build the bridge on May 7, 1954, and it opened to traffic on November 1, 1957. It unites the communities of Mackinaw City and St. Ignace. The main bridge cables are made from 42,000 miles of wire and the towers reach 554 feet above the water's surface. The current fare is $5 round-trip.

Aerial view of the Mackinac Bridge linking the Upper and Lower Peninsulas. Brian Walters

enforcement and order. The state civil rights commission redoubled its efforts to end discrimination. By 1968, 19 cities had enacted housing ordinances prohibiting discrimination in the sale or rent of real estate. African Americans were elected or promoted to more prominent positions in government, such as police and fire departments. Flint and Ypsilanti elected African Americans as mayors, and in 1974 Coleman A. Young was elected mayor of Detroit.

THE "RUSTBELT" STATE

In October of 1973, Syria and Egypt launched military attacks on Israel, starting a war that lasted less than three

The Motown Museum

The Motown Historical Museum was founded in 1985 and is one of Detroit's most popular tourist destinations. Its mission is to preserve the legacy of the Motown Record Corporation to educate and motivate people through exhibitions and programs. It is located on West Grand Boulevard in the original building that was purchased by former autoworker Berry Gordy. Begun in 1959 and christened "Hitsville, USA" by founder Berry Gordy, the museum exhibits trace the evolution of the Motown label and its tremendous impact on popular culture and musical styles in the Twentieth Century. Nostalgic collections of photographs, costumes, and music grace the exhibits. Visitors can stand in the original Studio A, which recorded so many of Motown's greatest hits.

weeks. The consequences of this conflict had a devastating effect on the United States in general and Michigan in particular. To show their support for Syria and Egypt, the Arab oil-producing countries in the Middle East imposed an oil embargo on the United States because of its pro-Israel policies. Gasoline prices skyrocketed, resulting in a world economic recession. By 1974 US oil prices had jumped 350 percent over the previous year, causing an energy crisis.

Motor vehicle sales plunged, causing massive layoffs among auto workers and associated industries, although the numbers were not as bad as the 1930s. The enormous rise in gas prices also caused car buyers to turn to smaller, less expensive, and more fuel efficient automobiles. Such fuel efficiency was an area to which Michigan-based American auto companies had not bothered to give much attention, but foreign producers, such as the Japanese, had been emphasizing it for years. Imported vehicle sales rose to over 18 percent of all sales in the United States by 1975, and sales of Nissan cars exceeded those of Volkswagen for the first time ever.

Then in the spring of 1979, a revolution in Iran sent the world back into a recession. Gas prices topped the one dollar mark and stayed there, hurting the sales of all cars

Coleman A. Young (1918-1997)

Born in Alabama, Coleman Young came to Detroit with his parents in 1923. After graduating from Eastern High School, he began a career of union and civil rights work that parallels the history of both subjects before entering politics. Elected a state senator in 1964, he was made Democratic floor leader and became the first African-American member of the Democratic National Committee in 1968. In 1973 he became the first African-American mayor of Detroit and served five successive terms in that office.

while propelling Japan to the number one spot of the world's automobile producers by 1980.

For Michigan, this new recession was the most severe shock to its economy since the Great Depression. Unemployment in the state reached 17 percent by March, 1982, nearly double the national average. A total of 725,000 people were out of work. Michigan had to borrow money from the federal government to meet its obligations to the unemployed.

Although all of the auto companies posted huge losses, the attention focused on Ford and Chrysler, which had the biggest. It was muttered in more than one meeting that neither company would survive much longer, but attention to detail began to turn both companies around. Changes in management at the highest levels and more enlightened leadership, along with some severe belt-tightening, saw the industry confound the experts and begin to make its way back to profits.

11

MODERN MICHIGAN

The wild fluctuations of the economy from the seventies through the early nineties provided a hard lesson for Michigan: the crying need for a more diverse economic base. The state could no longer count on the auto industry alone to provide the level of economic support that it had in the early decades of the twentieth century. Foreign competition, plant closings, and other shifts in the industry have convinced most people that the auto industry would not come back bigger than it was before, and that realization has opened the way for a more diverse economy.

POLITICS

Republicans have dominated state politics for most of the state's history. Beginning in the 1830s and out of loyalty to President Andrew Jackson for supporting Michigan statehood, the state's politics were Democrat and Jacksonian and remained so with two Whig exceptions until 1854 and the birth of the Republican Party. No Democrat was able to win election as governor until 1890.

That domination became so solidified by the 1900s that the state came close to one-party control. For a decade from 1918 to 1928, no Democrat was seated in the state senate and only nine served in the state house of representatives.

Progressivism and conservation managed to split the Republicans and allowed a Democrat, Woodbridge Ferris, to sit in 1912; Progressive support was so strong that Michigan voted for Theodore Roosevelt for president in 1912, as a third party candidate.

In 1921 the Republicans returned to Lansing with the election of Alexander J. Groesbeck for three terms, when two Democrats, William Comstock and Frank Murphy, rode Franklin Roosevelt's coattails into the governor's seat

The Gerber Baby

In 1927 national distribution of products was pretty much unheard of and that meant that foods would only be available in a few stores in certain areas of the country. The Gerbers, however, launched an advertising campaign featuring a money off coupon and the Gerber Baby, a face now known to millions of several generations of consumers. The ads appeared in periodicals such as *Good Housekeeping* and the AMA Journal. Grocers, at first skeptical, began placing orders by the dozen. But who was that cute face? People across the country have expressed their opinion, claiming it was Humphrey Bogart, Elizabeth Taylor, and even Bob Dole. But the baby's true identity is that of Ann Turner Cook, now a retired English teacher and mystery novelist. Dorothy Hope Smith, an artist specializing in children, submitted the unfinished charcoal drawing and Gerber executives were sold. The illustration became the official trademark in 1931.

in 1932 and 1936, respectively. Even though the state was carried by Owosso native Republican Thomas Dewey for president in 1948, voters put Democrat G. Mennen Williams in the governor's chair and a new era of Michigan politics began.

Governor "Soapy" Williams took office in 1949 and guided Michigan through the fabulous fifties, when the automobile industry in the state reached its apogee and those workers and employers enjoyed some very prosperous times. In fact, by the mid-1950s, Michigan enjoyed a per capita income among the highest in the world. This high standard of living enabled the state government to take an active role in the social and economic life of the state, building over 118,000 miles of roads and the Mackinac Bridge as well as establishing very generous welfare and educational programs. Governor Williams led a new coalition of voters consisting of labor leaders, recent immigrants, and African Americans to a level of overall prosperity unprecedented in the state's history. It also instituted an exuberant two-party political system that remains to this day.

But a good thing never lasts forever. In the early 1960s a small trickle of imported foreign cars began to make their way to America's highways. This trickle would eventually turn into a flood, sweeping away Michigan's preeminence in the auto industry and drowning the state in devastating recessions.

For twenty years, from 1963 to 1983, the Republicans held the governor's chair in the liberal person of George Romney and William Milliken (the longest serving governor at 14 years). Romney was a major force in rewriting the state constitution and in getting voter approval for it; he later faced major public criticism from no less a person than President Lyndon Johnson during the civil disturbance in Detroit in 1967.

The early 1980s saw the bottom drop out of Michigan's economy when two national recessions hit the state harder than any other because of the larger role played by the automobile industry. Economic anxiety along with social and racial tension from the 1960s and 1970s convinced voters to be skeptical of government, and the state gradually migrated from liberal to conservative political practices. Democratic Governor James J. Blanchard lost his bid for a third term in 1990 and Republican John Engler guided the state through the last decade of the century. He instituted many conservative policies, for example, eliminating General Assistance, doing away with the inheritance tax, and reforming other welfare programs. As the booming '90s ended, the state was broke and 2002 saw the inauguration of Jennifer Granholm.

PHARMACEUTICALS AND BIOTECH

Many have forgotten that Michigan's economy, both historically and present-day, has far greater diversity than anyone would imagine if one could only look beyond the Big Three. Many manufacturing activities are still taking place now as they have been since the middle of the nineteenth century. For example, Detroit's Parke-Davis & Company continues today as a division of pharmaceutical giant Warner-Lambert, with plants in several Michigan cities. Upjohn, founded some twenty years after Parke-

Davis, remains one of the foremost names in pharmaceuticals and a force in Kalamazoo's economy.

But Michigan has lost an estimated 200,000
manufacturing jobs since 1999 and that figure will no doubt
rise. State political and business leaders have been hard
pressed to find new industries to fill the void.

One area of help to an ailing economy is biotech
research, which goes hand in hand with the pharmaceutical
base already present in the state. The term "biotech" covers
everything from the laboratory development of medicines
to the merging of technology and science to produce an
array of medical devices. Michigan is one of the few states
in the country that can offer pharmaceutical firms
everything from top-quality research and the
manufacturing capabilities to make and sell the drugs. The
biotech industry in Michigan is considered by many of
those who study such things as still in its infancy.

One of the relatively new pharmaceutical giants to
Michigan is Pfizer, Inc., the world's largest drug maker,
which employs just under 10,000 people in Michigan. The
company maintains research labs in Ann Arbor, testing
facilities in the city of Kalamazoo, a farm for animal research
in Kalamazoo County, and production plants in Portage and
Holland, Michigan. There are about 600 smaller biotech and
pharmaceutical companies in Michigan, employing anywhere
from a handful to a thousand people each.

OTHER INDUSTRIES

Another industry that predates the automobile industry is
the chemical industry, and Dow Chemical, second in sales
only to DuPont, continues to make the Midland area one of
the world's important centers of manufacture and research.
In the same community, the Dow-Corning Corporation has
become the leading producer of silicones. Wyandotte
Chemical, the other Michigan chemical company of 1890s
origins, no longer exists as a separate business, but its
Michigan plants are still in operation as a part of the German
chemical firm BASF, having been acquired in 1969.

Not to be left out of the computer industry, the
Burrough's Corporation, a manufacturer of adding
machines in Detroit since 1904, acquired the Sperry
Company in 1986. The resulting corporation renamed itself

Cereal City

After 80 years of providing factory tours, Kellogg's closed their doors to the public. No longer could cereal fans see how their favorites were made. But now visitors can go into Kellogg's Cereal City USA, a theme attraction, factory tour, and museum all rolled into one. At Cereal City, you can travel along a simulated cereal production line and learn how Corn Flakes are made or take the self video tour where you get a free warm sample at the end. There is a grill/restaurant for the hungry and an outlet store for everything you need with a Kellogg's logo on it.

Unisys, and a number of its operations are still located in the Detroit area.

The largest major appliance manufacturer in the world is based in Benton Harbor. Beginning as the Upjohn Machine Company in 1911 making washing machines for Sears, Whirlpool began making machines under their new name in 1950. Fremont, Michigan, is home to Gerber Products, since 1973, the world's largest producer of baby foods. In 1994 Gerber was acquired by the Swiss company, Sandoz Ltd., which announced that it planned no major changes in the Fremont operation.

Alex Manoogian founded Masco Screw Products in Detroit in 1929 as an auto parts supplier and has taken that company in several different directions since. In 1954 he began manufacturing the single-handle faucet under the trade name Delta. In the 1980s, Masco moved in yet another direction, acquiring Henredon, Drexel Heritage, and other companies to become the country's largest furniture manufacturer and is still headquartered in Taylor, Michigan.

Michigan has long been an important center of the furniture business for well over one hundred years, and although the furniture styles that made Grand Rapids famous are things of the past, furniture of a different kind continues to put that area in the center of the industry. Shaw-Walker of Muskegon and American Seating of Grand Rapids by the 1980s had garnered control of 40 percent of the office-furnishing business. The leader in this industry since 1968 has been Steelcase of Grand Rapids, founded by Peter Wege in 1912.

Following behind Steelcase is Herman Miller, Inc., of Zeeland, founded in 1905, and Haworth, Inc., of Holland, founded in the late 1940s. These two companies are noted for their coordinated systems of office furnishings and are in terrific competition for second place. An important addition to the state's furniture companies in the 1920s was the Floral City Furniture Company of Monroe, Michigan. They soon after began making a reclining chair to which they gave the name "La-Z-Boy." Renaming the company in 1941, they have plants at sites across the country and around the world.

Perhaps no other Michigan business development of recent years can rival the Amway Corporation in its scope and in the financial rewards its founders have reaped. Richard M. DeVos and Jay Van Andel set up the company in Ada in 1959 and took the direct-selling technique to astronomical heights. By 1991 Amway had estimated sales of $3.9 billion through more than two million distributors, making it the largest direct-selling organization in the world. Still in private hands, Amway's founders have used their wealth in some ways to benefit the Grand Rapids area. The Amway Grand Hotel and Convention Center is but one demonstration of that largesse.

FOOD PROCESSING

Food processing is also one of Michigan's stable, flourishing industries. Just east of the Kalamazoo area is Kellogg's, the breakfast food leader and a thriving giant for Battle Creek since the 1890s. Fruit and vegetable canning companies have been in the state for decades. The Fremont Canning Company, in Fremont, Michigan, produced a line of such goods for its owners, Daniel and Dorothy Gerber. Their seven-month-old daughter, Sally, was being fed strained solid food, produced by hand in their own kitchen, until Dorothy decided that it could be done at the canning company a whole lot easier. One year later in late 1926, Gerber Baby Foods were ready for the national market. Today, Gerber distributes nearly 190 food products labeled in 16 different languages to 80 countries.

Aerial view of Round Island Lighthouse located in Lake Huron in the Straits area
Brian Walters

The Charles H. Wright Museum of African-American History

In 1965 Dr. Charles H. Wright established Detroit's first International Afro-American Museum, which opened its doors on West Grand Boulevard and very quickly outgrew its quarters. In 1978 a new facility went up on a plot of land between John R. and Brush, with students and a group of adults contributing to funding. Two more moves found the museum in a state of the art building on Warren Avenue, just east of Woodward, opening these doors on April 12, 1997. The museum strives to be a world-renowned history museum with outstanding collections and exhibits.

FRUITS AND VEGETABLES

Southwestern Michigan's temperate climate helps the state continue to be one of the nation's top producers of fruits and vegetables and, in fact, the leader in growing tart cherries and blueberries. The harvest season for most of these products lasts from June through October. In the summer, roadside markets and pick-your-own farms are never far away. Michigan is one of the top ten states for apples, sweet cherries, plums, grapes, pears, strawberries, peaches, asparagus, snap green beans, sweet corn, cauliflower, cucumbers, and wine. One can also find apricots, beets, blackberries, broccoli, cabbage, carrots, celery, melons, nectarines, sweet potatoes, pumpkins, and much more.

CONSERVATION AND PRESERVATION

As Michigan entered the last decade of the twentieth century, the fight to help preserve what it had was beginning. In 1990 the unemployment rate in the state was over nine percent and the state's population was rising slightly. New economic policies helped to create more than 800,000 new jobs, cutting that unemployment rate down to 3.4 percent in 2000. The state led the nation for an unprecedented five years in a row with the most new factories and expansion projects.

Stronger environmental laws ensured Michigan's position as a leader in protecting the Great Lakes, its vast amounts of freshwater, green spaces, and farmland. The state is also setting a good example in its attempts to reclaim brownfield sites.

As long ago as the middle of the nineteenth century, Michigan has had a history of environmental concern. In 1859 the first fisheries regulations were enacted in response to a depletion of fish stocks in Lake St. Clair and the Detroit River. The year 1887 saw Michigan become the first state to create the paid post of state game warden, followed two years later by an Independant Forestry Commission.

This century has also seen attempts to keep the environment clean. During the 1970s, several acts passed to protect Michigan's wonderland. The Environmental Protection Act, Great Lakes Shoreland Act, and the Inland Lakes and Streams Act were all part of an effort that continues today to keep the state itself healthy, and in the '80s and '90s these acts were strengthened, amended, and added to.

SPORTS

As dawn shed its meager light over the 1980s, things would change in Detroit sports. After years of habitual mediocrity, the Tigers gelled into an unbeatable team in 1984, the second team in Major League history to be in first place from the first day of the season to the last. After almost winning it all twice, the Pistons finally took their first of two successive NBA crowns. And in 1997, the Red Wings won the first of two successive Stanley Cups.

Sadly for most Detroit baseball fans, the Tigers ended 103 seasons at their ballpark, Tiger Stadium. They would start the 2000 season at Comerica Park, located on Woodward Avenue and right next to Ford Field, the new home of the Detroit Lions.

Baseball fans in other parts of the state were treated to new home town teams when the minor league Lansing Lugnuts began play in 1996 and the West Michigan Whitecaps played their first home game in April, 1994, in the Grand Rapids area. They've been crowned Midwest League Champions three times so far.

The Michigan Historical Museum

The flagship for the Michigan museum system is the Michigan Historical Museum, which is located in the Michigan Library and Historical Center in the state capitol, Lansing. The Michigan Historical Museum offers five levels of permanent and rotating exhibits that tell Michigan's story from the glaciers to the late twentieth century. Its exhibits include interactive computers, audio visual presentations, and hands-on elements that take the visitor from a prehistoric campsite, through Native American villages, and finally to the nineteenth century towns and cities of the state. There is a four-story atrium featuring a white pine and a three-story high topographical map of the state.

COOL CITIES

In 2001 the oldest city in the Midwest celebrated its 300th birthday. As Detroit enjoyed its year long party, several of its institutions found new life. From its humble beginnings on West Grand Boulevard in 1985, the Museum of African-American History has grown and evolved into the largest such museum in the world and is a new gem in the University Cultural Center of Detroit. The Dossin Great Lakes Museum on Belle Isle also showed an increase in interest as Michiganders celebrated their history anew.

In November of 2002, Michigan recorded another of its long, long list of firsts, though not the first in the country—the voters of the state elected their first woman as governor of the state of Michigan. Jennifer Mulhern Granholm will face her toughest challenges in the years ahead as the state must wrestle with a declining and increasingly poor urban population, increasing concern with quality of life, and an over dependence on the automobile industry.

In an ongoing effort to revitalize Michigan cities and neighborhoods and attract and retain jobs in the present and the future, Governor Granholm initiated the "Cool Cities" program in June, 2003. It is in part an urban strategy to revitalize communities, build community spirit, and retain knowledgeable workers and other creative class members who might otherwise leave the state to work elsewhere.

The first response was a success and 13 projects were underway in 2004 in nine Michigan cities: Battle Creek, Lansing, East Lansing, Kalamazoo, Detroit, Traverse City, Ann Arbor, and Holland. The 2005 designees are Ishpeming, Vassar, Grand Haven, Howell, Midland, Big Rapids, East Tawas, Romeo, Grass Lake, Iron River, Saginaw, Alpena, and Manistee. These programs will provide the catalyst for better main streets, downtowns, and neighborhoods across Michigan.

Award-Winning State

In a recent article posted on the state's website, Michigan is leading the nation in new corporate facilities and expansion, in the forefront of developing micro- and nanotechnology, and is recognized for its innovation in encouraging entrepreneurship.

According to Governor Granholm, these changes demonstrate how effectively Michigan is growing its advanced manufacturing base while also diversifying into new, high-tech industry centers. Granholm said, "Through Smart Zones, the Technology Tr-Corridor [meaning life sciences, advanced automotive technology, and homeland security], and other initiations, Michigan is establishing itself as a leader in the new industry sectors forming the foundation of the high-tech economy of the 21st Century."

Gradually and effectively, Michigan is branching out once again to many possibilities of good "health" that economic diversity can bring. Such health can be accomplished through new and innovative ideas teamed up with the old and established know-how of its people.

CHRONOLOGY OF MAJOR EVENTS

1622   Two French explorers, Etienne Brule and Grenoble, are the first white men to see Lake Superior.

1668   The first mission in Michigan is established at Sault Ste. Marie by Fathers Jacques Marquette and Claude Dablon.

1673   The first expedition to the Mississippi River leaves St. Ignace on May 17, led by Father Marquette, fur trader Louis Jolliet, and five voyageurs.

1701   French army officer Antoine de la Mothe Cadillac establishes a permanent post at le Detroit (the straits).

1715   Fort Michilimackinac is established by the French at the Straits of Mackinac.

1760   The French surrender Fort Ponchartrain to the British at the conclusion of the French and Indian War, ending French rule in Detroit.

1763   Ottawa Chief Pontiac leads an unsuccessful attempt to capture Detroit by siege.

1787   The Northwest Ordinance of 1787 is passed, defining the procedure for statehood in the Northwest Territory, of which Michigan is a part.

1792   The first election is held in Michigan, under the British Parliament's Constitutional Act.

1796   Soldiers of the 1st US Infantry Regiment arrive in Detroit to take over from the British in the Great Lakes region.

1805   The Territory of Michigan is created with Detroit as its capitol; William Hull is appointed governor, but before he arrives the town is completely destroyed by fire.

1807   The Treaty of Detroit is signed, ceding the southeastern quarter of the state to the United States; four chieftains are signatories.

1809   The first newspaper is issued in Michigan; *The Michigan Essay* is printed in French and English.

1812   War begins between England and the United States; Detroit and Fort Mackinac are surrendered to the British.

1813   In January, a small force of US troops is attacked and defeated by the British and their Native American allies at the River Raisin near Monroe, Michigan. Later that year, American forces reenter Detroit and defeat the British at the Battle of the Thames in Canada. Lewis Cass is appointed military and civil governor of the territory.

1819	The Treaty of Saginaw is signed, which cedes almost six million acres of Native American lands to Michigan settlers. Michigan sends a delegate to Congress.
1820	The first highway is built in Michigan, from Detroit to Ohio.
1822	Public stagecoaches begin service from Detroit.
1828	A territorial capitol building is constructed at Detroit.
1830	Stephen G. Simmons is hanged for murder in Detroit, the last execution in Michigan.
1835	Argument over the Michigan–Ohio border erupts into conflict; Michigan is denied statehood until it surrenders its claim and settles for the Upper Peninsula in exchange. First constitutional convention is held and Stevens T. Mason is elected governor.
1837	Michigan enters the Union as the 26th State.
1838	First public school district is organized in Detroit under the state public school law.
1841	Congress allocates funds for the construction of Fort Wayne at Detroit. African-American Methodists reorganize their church as African Methodist Episcopal Church in Detroit.
1842	Copper mining begins in earnest near Keweenaw Point.
1844	Iron ore is discovered near at Negaunee in the Upper Peninsula.
1847	First movement of the Underground Railroad to Michigan; Kentucky slaves arrive in Marshall, Michigan, at the home of Adam Crosswhite. By law, the state capitol will be located at Lansing in the center of the state.
1854	The Republican Party is formed at Jackson, Michigan.
1855	The Sault Canal is completed and opened for business, improving the shipping of mineral resources from the Upper Peninsula.
1859	Thomas Edison, of Port Huron, starts work as a newsboy on the railroad route.
1861–65	Civil War; Michigan sends over 90,000 soldiers to fight.
1867	Female taxpayers are allowed to vote in school elections in Michigan but must still wait for total suffrage.
1870	The word "white" is removed from the state constitution by voters; African-American residents can vote.
1871	First compulsory school attendance law is passed.
1877	First telephones are installed in Detroit; Frederick Stearnes Co. is first business to be connected.
1879	New State Capitol is dedicated in Lansing.
1881	The Detroit Baseball Club, organized in 1880, begins professional play in the National League.
1883	First incandescent lights are used in Detroit.

1896	Charles Brady King of Detroit successfully test drives his gasoline powered automobile on Detroit streets. Three months later, Henry Ford follows suit.
1900	First woman, Alice Chaney of Detroit, licensed as a Great Lakes ship pilot.
1901	Detroit celebrates its bicentennial; Henry Ford Company founded.
1903	Ford Motor Co., Buick, and Packard founded or organized in Detroit.
1905	Ty Cobb begins his Major League career.
1908	General Motors organized; Ford builds first Model T; Fisher Body Co. organized.
1909	First mile of concrete pavement laid in Detroit over a stretch of Woodward Ave between Seven Mile and Eight Mile Roads. Construction begins on the Highland Park Ford plant; first vehicle to roll out next year.
1910	First primary election held in Michigan.
1911	Chevrolet Motor Co. founded; state flag adopted, with seal; white lines are painted on roads to control traffic.
1913	Ford begins moving assembly line at Highland Park plant.
1914	Ford institutes the $5 a day wage.
1917	Michigan women can vote in presidential elections.
1920	WWJ begins commercial broadcasting of regular radio programs in Detroit, the first in the nation.
1929	The Ambassador Bridge opens to traffic from Detroit to Windsor, Ontario, and back again.
1930	The Detroit-Windsor Auto Tunnel opens for business.
1933	Michigan is the first state to vote for national prohibition repeal.
1935	The United Auto Workers organize in Detroit as part of the CIO. The Detroit Tigers, Lions, and Red Wings win their respective world championships, making Detroit the "City of Champions."
1936	Workers stage a sit-down strike at GM plants in Flint, Michigan.
1941	Auto plants are converted to war production and Michigan becomes known as the "Arsenal of Democracy."
1946	Network of Detroit freeways in planning stages: Fisher, Lodge, and Chrysler freeways will radiate from Detroit.
1950	Ruth Thompson, of Muskegon, is the first Michigan woman elected to US Congress.
1952	Cora Mae Brown of Detroit is first black woman elected to Michigan senate.
1954	Northland, the nation's first large regional shopping center, opens.

1957	Mackinac Bridge opens to traffic.
1959	Berry Gordy founds Motown Records in Detroit.
1963	Michigan voters approve new state constitution.
1965	Michigan's first astronaut in space, James McDivitt, takes flight in Gemini.
1967	Riots erupt in Detroit.
1973	State Senator Coleman A. Young is elected Detroit's first black mayor.
1974	Gerald R. Ford of Grand Rapids becomes the 38th president of the United States.
1976	Michigan enacts bottle law (deposit of $.10 each)
1977	Renaissance Center and the Science Center open in Detroit.
1980	The Republican National Convention is held in Detroit.
1982	Super Bowl XVI is held in Pontiac Silverdome.
1987	Michigan celebrates 150 years of statehood.
1989	Detroit Pistons win NBA Championship.
1990	Pistons repeat.
1992	The Scenic River Act passed, protecting areas along 14 Michigan rivers from development.
1993	Dennis Archer elected mayor of Detroit to succeed Young.
1997	Detroit Red Wings win first Stanley Cup since 1955.
1998	Red Wings repeat.
1999	Detroit Tigers play last game at Michigan and Trumbull (since 1896).
2000	Tigers play their first game at new park, Comerica.
2001	Detroit celebrates its tercentenary.
2002	Michigan elects its first female governor, Jennifer M. Granholm.
2003	Michigan Governor Granholm initiates "Cool Cities" program.
2004	The Detroit Pistons win NBA Championship.

Cultural Highlights

Film

Michigan has been the setting for a number of motion pictures, from the beautiful country backgrounds of the Upper Peninsula to the gritty backdrop of the Motor City. Here are a few examples:

8 Mile. A movie featuring Detroit native hip-hop artist Eminem that explores life in inner-city Detroit.

Anatomy of a Murder. This 1959 thriller is set in the U.P. and starred Jimmy Stewart.

Escanaba in Da Moonlight. A Jeff Daniels 2000 film that makes a lot of fun of "Yoopers," or people from the Upper Peninsula.

Hoffa. A 1992 movie starring Danny DeVito and Jack Nicholson based on the life and disappearance of labor leader Jimmy Hoffa.

Grosse Pointe Blank. A 1997 movie starring John Cusack as a Grosse Pointe High School alumni turned hit man.

Renaissance Man. This 1994 movie starred Danny DeVito and had great scenes shot in Detroit.

Roger and Me. A 1989 documentary about the effects on a small town totally dependant on a large company similar to GM.

Somewhere in Time. A beautiful movie set on Mackinac Island with the Grand Hotel as the backdrop, this love story starred Christopher Reeves.

Super Sucker. Another Jeff Daniels film doing the same thing for Jackson, Michigan (2002).

Tucker: The Man and His Dream. A 1988 film based on the life of the designer of the Tucker automobile, starring Jeff Bridges and set in Ypsilanti, Michigan.

Books

Michigan has had its share of authors, such as Ernest Hemingway, Robert Travers, and Bruce Catton. Some of the books with a Michigan setting are:

Catton, Bruce. *Waiting for the Morning Train*. 1972. Known primarily for his Civil War works, this story is about growing up in Benzonia, Michigan around the turn of the century.

Travers, Robert. *Anatomy of a Murder*. 1958. A bestseller set in Marquette County, the riveting story of a murder trial that put the Upper Peninsula on the map.

Travers, Robert. *Trout Madness*. 1960. A nonfiction book about the passion for fishing.

Piercy. Marge. *Braided Lives.* 1982. A fiction account of a woman writer set in Detroit, Ann Arbor and New York City.

Stocking, Kathleen. *Letters From the Leelanau.* 1990. A nonfiction collection of essays about the people and places in Leelanau County.

Hamper, Ben. *Rivethead.* 1991. An autobiography of a Flint, Michigan "shop-rat." A vivid portrait of life in a factory town.

Music

Music has been an integral part of custom and culture in Michigan since the Native American inhabitants chanted their prayers and sang to the stroke of their canoe paddles. The French and English brought their musical tradition with them as well as the Eastern colonist from New York and Pennsylvania, who followed after 1800.

In the late nineteenth century, a former milkman, Jerome H. Remick, obtained controlling interest in a music publishing company in Detroit. By the early 1900s he had offices in New York City and would build his company into the world's largest with several million-selling songsheets. By the 1920s, scores of songwriters in Tin Pan Alley could call Saginaw home.

One aspect of Michigan's musical contribution that is always overlooked is that which took place between 1966 and 1972 in the history of modern rock music. In thousands of basements and garages across Southeastern Michigan groups of musicians, long-haired and not, pounded on drums and twanged electric guitars in a loud form of rebellion. Not surprisingly, there were a number of successes: Mitch Ryder and the Detroit Wheels, the MC5, Amboy Dukes, The Rationals, Bob Seger, Frost, Savage Grace and Frijid Pink; Ann Arbor's Commander Cody, Flint's Grand Funk Railroad, Ted Nugent and Glen Frey of the Eagles. And who could forget the journal of rock 'n' roll: *Creem* magazine roaring out of Detroit in 1969?

SPECIAL EVENTS

The exact dates below reflect the events as scheduled in 2005–2006.

JANUARY

Cirque: Dreams—January 3–4—Dow Event Center, Saginaw.
The Russian National Ballet—January 7—The Whiting, Flint.
Plymouth International Ice Sculpture Spectacular—January
     12–16—Plymouth.
Heikinpaiva Mid-Winter Festival—January 20–22—Hancock.

FEBRUARY

Movers & Shakers: Michigan Immigrants and Migrants—February
     6–October 9—Lansing.
Winter Carnival—February 8–11—Calumet.
Perchville, USA—February 10–12—Tawas City.

MARCH

Beehive—March 3–12—State Theater, Bay City.
Clare's Irish Festival—March 14–18—Clare.
St. Patrick's Day Parade—March 19—Bay City.

APRIL

Four Cylinder Enduro Auto Races—April 1–November 4—
     Kalamazoo.
Fortieth Anniversary Celebration—April 15–October 29—
     Windmill Island, Holland.
Durand Union Station Centennial Celebration—April 17–
     September 25—Durand.
Vermontville Maple Syrup Festival—April 28–30—Lansing.

MAY

Tulip Time Festival—May 6–13—Holland.
The World Expo of Beer—May 19–20—Frankenmuth.
Michigan Week—May 20–26—Lansing.

JUNE

Charlevoix Farmer's Market—June 1–October 26—Charlevoix.
Frankenmuth Bavarian Festival—June 8–11—Frankenmuth.
The Place of Our Ancestor—June 17–18—Chesaning.
Cars, Coney, Mott & More—June 19–April 23—Flint.
Jam and Open Mic Night—June 22–December 20—Coopersville
     Farm Museum.

Fraternity, Charity and Loyalty: Treasures of the Grand Army of the Republic—June 22–January 7—Jackson.
Michigan Challenge Balloon Festival—June 23–25—Howell.

JULY

National Cherry Festival—July 1–18—Traverse City.
Fourth of July Celebration—July 4—Mackinac Island.
Coast Guard Festival—July 28–August 6—Grand Haven.

AUGUST

Saginaw County Fair—August 1–5—Saginaw.
Renaissance Festival—August 13–September 25—Holly.
Upper Peninsula State Fair—August 14–20—Escanaba.
Michigan State Fair—August 28–September 5—Detroit.

SEPTEMBER

Paw Paw Wine and Harvest Festival—September 9—Paw Paw.
One World Groove—September 22–May 18—Arab–American National Museum, Dearborn.
Hillsdale County Fair—September 25–October 1—Hillsdale.
Pumpkin Festival—September 30–October 2—Zeeland.

OCTOBER

Frankenmuth Oktoberfest—October 1–31—Frankenmuth.

NOVEMBER

Holiday Open House—November 4–6—Tecumseh.
Yuletide, 2005—November 11–13—Blissfield.
Holland Winterfest—November 25–December 10—Holland.
Horse & Buggy Rides—November 25–December 16—Allegan.
Dickens Olde Fashioned Christmas Festival—November 25–December 18—Holly.
Singing Christmas Tree—November 30–December 2—Muskegon.

DECEMBER

See November events.

Contact Information

www.authors.libraryofmichigan.org—Great database on everything to do with Michigan associated writers.

www.detroitsports.com—All the info on Detroit's professional sports teams.

www.lansinglugnuts.com—Rosters, schedules, history of this minor league team.

www.michigan.gov—For anything you want to know about the state.

www.michiganinthewar.org—An excellent site for Michigan's Civil War history.

www.whitecaps-baseball.com—Same for this western team.

Bridge in County Park, Battle Creek
Willard Library

Sources and Further Reading

Armour, David and Keith Widder. *At the Crossroads: Michilimackinac During the American Revolution*. Mackinac Island, MI: Mackinac Island State Park Commission, 1986.

Bak, Richard. *Detroit Across Three Centuries*. Chelsea, MI: Sleeping Bear Press, 2001.

Baldwin, Neil. *Henry Ford and the Jews: The Mass Production of Hate*. New York: Public Affairs, 2001.

Barnard, John. *American Vanguard: The United Auto Workers During the Reuther Years, 1935–1970*. Detroit: Wayne State University Press, 2004.

Bogue, Margaret Beattie. *Fishing the Great Lakes: An Environmental History, 1783–1933*. Madison: University of Wisconsin Press, 2000.

Brehm, Victoria, ed. *The Women's Great Lakes Reader*. Duluth, MN: Holy Cow! Press, 1998.

Brinkley, Douglas. *Wheels For the World: Henry Ford, His Company, and a Century of Progress*. New York: Viking, 2003.

Capeci, Donald J. Jr., ed. *Detroit and the "Good War": The World War II Letters of Mayor Edward Jeffries and Friends*. Lexington, KY: University of Kentucky Press, 1996.

Carson, Gerald. *Cornflake Crusade*. New York: Rinehart, 1957.

Catton, Bruce. *Michigan: A Bicentennial History*. New York: W.W. Norton, 1976.

Cleland, Charles E. *Rites of Conquest: The History and Culture of Michigan's Native Americans*. Ann Arbor: University of Michigan Press, 1992.

Clifton, James A., George L. Cornell, and James M. McClurken. *People of the Three Fires: The Ottawa, Potawatomi and Ojibway of Michigan*. Grand Rapids, MI: Grand Rapids Inter-Tribal Council, 1986.

Clive, Alan. *State of War: Michigan in World War II*. Ann Arbor: University of Michigan Press, 1979.

Dixon, David. *Never Come to Peace Again: Pontiac's Uprising and the Fate of the British Empire in North America*. Norman, OK: University of Oklahoma Press, 2005.

Dowd, Gregory. *War Under Heaven: Pontiac, the Indian Nations, and the British Empire*. Baltimore, MD: Johns Hopkins University Press, 2002.

Dunbar, Willis F. *All Aboard! A History of Railroads in Michigan*. Grand Rapids, MI: W.B. Eerdmans Pub. Co., 1969.

Dunbar, Willis F., and George S. May. *Michigan: A History of the Wolverine State*. 3rd Rev. Ed. Grand Rapids, MI: W.B.

Eerdmans Pub. Co., 1995.

Dunningan, Brian. *Frontier Metropolis: Picturing Early Detroit, 1701–1838*. Detroit: Wayne State University Press, 2001.

Fine, Sidney. *Sit-down: The General Motors Strike of 1936–1937*. Ann Arbor: University of Michigan Press, 1969.

Fine, Sidney. *Violence in the Model City: The Cavanagh Administration, Race Relations, and the Detroit Riot of 1967*. Ann Arbor: University of Michigan Press, 1989.

Gilpin, Alec R. *The Territory of Michigan, 1805–1837*. East Lansing: Michigan State University Press, 1970.

Gilpin, Alec R. *The War of 1812 in the Old Northwest*. East Lansing: Michigan State University Press, 1958.

Gray, Susan. *The Yankee West: Community Life on the Michigan Frontier*. Chapel Hill: University of North Carolina Press, 1996.

Halsey, John, ed. and Michael Stafford, assoc. ed. *Retrieving Michigan's Buried Past: The Archeology of the Great Lakes State*. Bloomfield Hills, MI: Cranbrook Institute of Science, 1999.

Holli, Melvin G. *Reform in Detroit: Hazen S. Pingree and Urban Politics*. New York: Oxford University Press, 1969.

Hyde, Charles K. and colored photographs by Ann and John Mahan. *The Northern Lights: Lighthouses of the Upper Great Lakes*. Detroit: Wayne State University Press, 1995.

Hyde, Charles K. *Riding the Roller Coaster: The History of the Chrysler Corporation*. Detroit: Wayne State University Press, 2003.

Karamanski, Theodore J. *Deep Woods Frontier: A History of Logging in Northern Michigan*. Detroit: Wayne State University Press, 1989.

Katzman, David M. *Before the Ghetto: Black Detroit in the Nineteenth Century*. Urbana: University of Illinois Press, 1973.

Kestenbaum, Justin L., ed. *The Making of Michigan, 1820–1860: A Pioneer Anthology*. Detroit: Wayne State University Press, 1990.

Kilar, Jeremy W. *Michigan's Lumbertowns: Lumbermen and Laborers in Saginaw, Bay City, and Muskegon, 1870–1905*. Detroit: Wayne State University Press, 1990.

Klunder, Willard Carl. *Lewis Cass and the Politics of Moderation*. Keny, OH: Kent State University Press, 1996.

Lichtenstein, Nelson. *The Most Dangerous Man in Detroit: Walter Reuther and the Fate of American Labor*. New York: Basic Books, 1995.

Mason, Philip P. *Rumrunning and the Roaring Twenties: Prohibition on the Michigan-Ohio Waterway*. Detroit: Wayne State University Press, 1995.

May, George S. *A Most Unique Machine: The Michigan Origins of the American Automobile Industry*. Grand Rapids, MI: W.E. Eerdmans Pub. Co., 1974.

Poremba, David Lee, ed. *Detroit in its World Setting: A Three Hundred Year Chronology, 1701–2001*. Detroit: Wayne State University Press, 2001.

Poremba, David Lee. *Detroit: A Motor City History*. Charleston, SC: Arcadia, 2001.

Romig, Walter. *Michigan Place Names: The History of the Founding and the Naming of More Than Five Thousand Past and Present Michigan Communities*. Detroit: Wayne State University Press, 1986.

Sugure, Thomas J. *The Origins of the Urban Crisis: Race and Inequality in Postwar Detroit*. Princeton: Princeton University Press, 1996.

Tanner, Helen Hornbeck, ed. *Atlas of Great Lakes Indian History*. Norman: University of Oklahoma Press, 1987.

Thompson, Mark L. *Steamboats and Sailors of the Great Lakes*. Detroit: Wayne State University Press, 1991.

Thurner, Arthur W. *Strangers and Sojourners: A History of Michigan's Keweenaw Peninsula*. Detroit: Wayne State University Press, 1994.

Vanderhill, C. Warren. *Settling the Great Lakes Frontier: Immigration to Michigan, 1837–1924*. Lansing: Michigan Historical Commission, 1970.

Weeks, George. *Stewards of the State: The Governors of Michigan*. 2nd rev. ed. Detroit: *Detroit News*, Ann Arbor: Historical Society of Michigan, 1991.

White, Richard. *The Middle Ground: Indians, Empires, and Republics in the Great Lakes Region, 1650–1815*. Cambridge: Cambridge University Press, 1991.

Woodford, Arthur. *This Is Detroit, 1701–2001*. Detroit: Wayne State University Press, 2001.

Zunz, Olivier. *The Changing Face of Inequality: Urbanization, Industrial Development and Immigrants to Detroit, 1880–1920*. Chicago: University of Chicago Press, 1982.